Patricia Cleghorn is Principal of Orchid International providing Personal Focus programmes for business, and of The Self-Esteem Company providing seminars for the public. Having worked with individuals, groups and major businesses for many years, she has an exceptionally wide range of experience in helping people to build self-esteem, self-motivation and success.

THE SECRETS OF SELF-ESTEEM

MAKE THE CHANGES YOU WANT IN YOUR LIFE

PATRICIA CLEGHORN

vega

ISBN 1-84333-142-X

A catalogue record for this book is available from the British Library

First published in 2002 by
Vega
64 Brewery Road
London, N7 9NT

A member of the Chrysalis Group plc

Visit our website at www.chrysalisbooks.co.uk

Printed in Great Britain by CPD, Wales

This book is dedicated to you, the reader.

Thank you to my family, friends, people on our programmes and my colleagues for your continuing interest and enthusiasm.

Contents

SECTION EIGHT
Review and Forward Focus

AUTHOR'S NOTE

You can first read right through the book or just those sections you are most drawn to. However, for maximum benefit, after you have read each part, do the short *Personal Focus* exercises at the end and also remind yourself of the helpful thoughts that are included.

These self-esteem thoughts throughout the book are suggestions to help you think in a way which is beneficial to you. You can read them over once or twice as you go through the book. The more often you remind yourself of helpful thoughts, the more confident about yourself and your life you will become. As you proceed, you can vary them in a way that feels right to you, and make up your own helpful thoughts.

As you progress through the book, putting the suggestions that you choose into practice will help you greatly. Your perspective will change from when you start the book to when you have completed it. You'll become more joyful and experience your ability to succeed with what is important to you. You will learn to really value yourself.

SECTION ONE

Build Your Self-Esteem

CHAPTER ONE

Build Your Self-Esteem

Do you at times feel hesitant and lacking in confidence, wanting to make changes and to feel happier, but not knowing how? Are you an outwardly confident and successful person, yet feeling a lack of joy and real direction in your life? You may be surprised to hear that this is an excellent starting point. Having the feeling that you want to be more confident or that something is missing from your life can be a spur to help you move forward. You are not alone in feeling low self-esteem: nearly everyone does at some time. Self-doubt and relationship problems are directly traceable to low self-esteem. If you're feeling your life is out of control as a result of rapid and unexpected changes, developing self-esteem will help you to feel a sense of control and balance. On a daily basis you will be better able to make the best use of your time and energy. You will be able to focus on what is important to you in your life, whatever your age and current circumstances.

When you are with people who are self-confident and seem comfortable with themselves you may wonder what the secret of their self-esteem is.

You may have been thinking that someone or something outside of yourself could give you high self-esteem. What do you imagine will give you more self-worth? You may wish that you were more successful, more attractive, younger or more popular. Maybe you are anxious to meet the right person, or to improve your current relationship. You may be experiencing insecurity or simply be feeling that there is something missing in your life.

We would all love a magic wand to be waved for us. That's not going to happen, but the good news is that you can make the magic in your own life. Even while wanting a more satisfying life you can start to respect yourself right away. This means treating yourself well instead of harshly. Respect for yourself also involves identifying what you need and want, what is right for you as an individual. Being gentle with yourself applies not just to such things as ensuring you don't push yourself to the point of exhaustion but in how you speak about yourself to others and, importantly, how you speak to yourself in your head. For many people, the sorts of things they say to themselves would be unacceptable coming from someone else.

I am starting to respect and like myself more.

STOP CRITICIZING AND START APPRECIATING YOURSELF

A first step is to notice when you're being self-critical. Be aware of that inner voice on a 'critical binge' going on and on, putting yourself down, saying things like 'I'm hopeless, I'll never, I can't, I'm so stupid, why didn't I, if only I'd . . .'. You can let this self-critical voice continue throughout the day and end up feeling really low. Instead, decide to say 'Stop! Enough. What I actually like about myself for example, my warmth with friends, my patience, my courage, my sense of humour, my good dress sense, and how sensitively I coped with that difficult person'. Someone on a recent course said that he realized if he spoke to his friends as he spoke to himself he wouldn't have any friends! You have many good points: you'll feel so much better and be so much more effective too, both in your personal life and at work, if you appreciate yourself more. The bonus in appreciating yourself is that you become less dependent upon other people's appreciating you. This in turn can make them more inclined to do so! Appreciating yourself is much less stressful than criticizing yourself all the time.

It may feel odd at first to focus on how well you are doing instead of noticing what you haven't done or might have done differently. At the end of each working day take a moment, instead of mentally reviewing all you *haven't* done, to appreciate what you *have* achieved. Then, in those moments when you're on your own and feel you need extra encouragement and someone to be nice to you, you can be appreciative and supportive of yourself.

I appreciate myself.

ACCEPTING YOURSELF HELPS YOU MAKE CHANGES

You don't need to postpone liking and accepting yourself. Very often we feel if we only lost *x* pounds in weight or gained £*x* then we'd be halfway acceptable. Being human we all want to feel liked and accepted by other people. It is natural that you will want that for yourself and enjoy having that happen. However, the most important person for you to have acceptance from is yourself. It is very difficult for others to like and accept you as you are when you are unaccepting of yourself. If you find yourself unacceptable and unlikeable in certain aspects, deliberately focus on what you do like about yourself.

Accepting and liking yourself feels good and will actually assist you in leading the best life you can imagine for yourself. Being compassionate to and understanding of yourself won't make you lazy. It's easier to make the changes you want when you support and encourage yourself. So don't postpone liking yourself and feeling good until you've made the desired alterations to yourself and your life! You will more easily obtain your goals with regard to, for example, body weight, degree of fitness, progress in your work and greater harmony in your relationships, when you accept yourself as you are as the starting point. Your own self-acceptance is a friend you will want to have for life!

It is becoming easier for me to accept myself.

START APPROVING OF YOURSELF

Break the habit of disapproval! It's the easiest thing in the world to be disapproving of yourself. This is especially so when you feel you should be somehow different from the way you are right now, for example, getting more done more quickly, to have made more progress with your career or to have handled a relationship better. Often there need not be any particular reason; we just disapprove of ourselves anyway. However much you may be presenting an 'I'm all right, there's nothing the matter with me' face to the world, you can often be actually disapproving of and disliking yourself. This is not surprising because whether or not we have been brought up with full material comforts we are rarely taught to approve of or respect ourselves. The habit of disapproving of ourselves usually comes from years of not feeling worthy, not feeling approved of by others and from being judgmental and harsh with ourselves. You can spend a great deal of time worrying about whether people in general or certain particular people approve of you. Very often we waste time worrying about this disapproval when it may not even exist. A supposedly stern look on a person's face can sometimes just signify that they are thinking about what they are going to have for tea! Also we can be really worried that a boss at work is disapproving of us in a meeting. What does his serious look mean? It may well mean that he is concerned about the impression he is making. Just think, the person whose approval you're so worried about getting, may be worrying about getting your approval! So relax and approve of yourself.

Approve of yourself at all times and in all circumstances, for you are the most important person in your own life. Approve of yourself even when you want things to be different. Particularly approve of yourself when you fear another person may not or when you've just made a mistake then you can correct or let go of it more easily. We can't *make* other people approve of us; you may be able to recall a time when you have tried that. What you can do, however, is to step up your own level of approval. You'll find it interesting that as you do this other people seem to approve of you more anyway!

I approve of myself even when I wish I'd done things differently.

GIVE YOURSELF PERMISSION TO MOVE FORWARD

Think of the times you've held yourself back because you weren't sure if you had another person's approval. A young secretary on one of our programmes, who came from a strict family background, wanted to change to doing something she really loved and that was to be a freelance makeup artist for television. To do this she needed further training. Support was not forthcoming from her family so she really had to approve of herself and give herself permission to move forward. She had the courage to do this, winning a prize for best student, and her new career got under way successfully. Is there something that you would love to do in your life that you're holding back on because you don't feel that you have sufficient approval? First decide if it's something that you'd love to do and whether it would be of benefit to you. Then give yourself permission to move forward. You may wait a long time if you are waiting for someone else's approval, and with the encouragement of your own support the practical steps are easier to take.

YOU CAN STOP WORRYING

We all know that worrying about something won't make it any better and it will probably make us feel a lot worse. However, that doesn't stop us doing it if it's a habit, and it is for most people. Try adding up all the time you spend worrying each week. Has worrying all this time made you feel any better? Has it proved at all helpful? Repetitive worry is a waste of energy.

When you start to worry about the past, let go where possible. When you start worrying about the future, see the difference between going over and over something and a genuine concern that you can pay attention to and take action upon. Very often our worries about the future are unfounded. For example, in a work situation where several people feared the effects of forthcoming changes, there was a general air of despondency, a lack of motivation and negativity. One of the people concerned realized they were pulling each other down and started to be more positive, raising the energy level and expectations of the whole group. In the event, the organizational changes were beneficial, as individuals within the group became more positive, flexible and open to new opportunities. So when you notice that you are wasting time and pulling yourself down by worrying, then stop. Decide you'll change this habit. You can set aside a time each day which is going to be your 'worry time', say 6.30 in the evening, and you worry then for ten minutes. Each time during the day when you start to worry you postpone it until that time. It becomes less attractive to worry when you've got to! When the worry wears off, remember to cancel your worry time so that your mind doesn't continue this!

As I stop worrying I have more time and energy.

LET GO OF BLAMING YOURSELF

Do you find you're continually blaming yourself? This is not supportive of your self-esteem as you will suffer from guilt and low-level anxiety. While you may choose to act different-ly in the future, even to communicate your apologies or regret to another person, it does not help you in the least to continuously go over the past, blaming and putting yourself down, feeling that you're a bad person.

There is always a choice in present time of how you behave or act, yet it's not helpful to blame yourself for what you see as mistakes, omissions, wrong choices in the past. At some level you're usually doing the best you are able to. It is always with hindsight and in retrospect that you feel you could have done better.

If blaming yourself has become a habit, if you keep feeling that everything is your fault, notice how upset you feel, how depressed going over these thoughts makes you. Gently release yourself from those unhelpful thoughts. Let go and tell yourself that you are starting to stop blaming yourself and to stop making yourself wrong.

I now stop blaming myself and choose peace of mind.

Nothing you've done will be helped by your going over and over it, agonizing and blaming yourself. It's unlikely either that anything you've ever done is so awful that you need to beat yourself up about it time and time again. Focus instead on what is important and joyful for you.

LISTEN TO YOURSELF – YOU KNOW WHAT IS BEST FOR YOU

It is appropriate for your self-esteem to put your attention on what matters to you. Listening to yourself, to what is best for you, is the beginning of developing your personal intuition, that infallible guide to what is right for you as a unique individual. You are already using this when you have a 'hunch' about something, when you have a 'feeling' that it's important to do something.

You probably remember times when you've followed your hunches, and things have gone easily and effortlessly. At other times you might have had a good idea and reasoned yourself out of it and then had to come back to it months later!

If you are nervous of following through on your personal intuition, start with something small – which book to buy, for example – where there is no pressure from yourself or anyone else to get it right. You can then test it out on bigger things as you feel more confident with it.

You Deserve to be Happy

You deserve to be happy. You are not here to suffer. Yet sometimes you may notice that when you're happy and contented at least for some continuous period of time you find yourself wondering if it's too good to be true. It's too big a contrast with when you feel low. It's important to realize that being joyful is your natural state, your natural self-esteem state. You may also feel that if only your circumstances were different you would feel more joyful, but this isn't necessarily the case. You don't need to wait. Notice that you can decide to feel joyful right away. You have a choice in how you feel and you have to find out for yourself what will make you happy and then put it in place.

So often we want others to give us attention, in order that we might feel happier, for example. We need to do this for ourselves. It is freeing for you and the other person. It is important to understand that no one else can take responsibility for your happiness long-term nor you for theirs. So you might like to say today when you finish any task that must be done, 'What could I do that would feel good and joyful for me?'

A young woman was very disgruntled and angry about

various aspects of her life, angry with other people and with herself. As she started to treat herself better, to give herself more of what she wanted, to ask herself what she could do for herself, she started to feel lighter and more content.

A mother with young children always put everything else first and herself last. She constantly felt that she wasn't important and couldn't do the things she wanted to do. As she began to look for ways she could treat herself better on a daily basis and ask for the help she needed, she felt less tired and was able to look long-term at what she wanted as well as enjoying her children.

Doing what is good for you and gives you joy in fact makes you less needy and less demanding. Keeping yourself feeling happy doesn't make you any less caring, compassionate and truly helpful with others. The reverse tends to be true; you're much more contented and more pleasant to be with.

When I do what is good for me everyone benefits.

DECIDE TO TREAT YOURSELF WELL

You wouldn't deliberately treat someone else badly, would you? In fact we can be quite good at working out what would be nice for other people, organizing surprises, buying treats and doing things for them. Yet we are very often harsh with ourselves, not pausing to see how we can treat ourselves well. Especially when you are under pressure, it's common sense to treat yourself gently and not decide, for example, to paint the hall right away when you've got an important deadline to meet at work. This same principle applies in all areas of your life, so just look on a daily basis at what can you do that is kind to yourself.

I now treat myself as well as I treat other people.

Treating yourself well is part of having high self-esteem.

Being harsh and punishing yourself never makes you feel better. However, you may just not have thought about what is best for you. Even when you're busy it's important to spend some time doing things you enjoy. You may like your work and care for your family, yet having time off, doing what you really want, is important. There may be ways you can be nicer to yourself with regard to your body, for example not pushing yourself to the point of exhaustion. Do you make sure you spend time with supportive people who are fun, not just those whom you can help and support? Especially when you're busy it's important to treat yourself well and be gentle with yourself.

As you are now developing higher self-esteem by practising, expect improvements right away. You will already be noticing that you think and feel better about yourself and your life. You can remember the three As of self-esteem building – appreciate yourself, accept yourself and approve of yourself. As you start to let go of blaming yourself and learn to worry less you will have far more energy. Keep listening to your hunches, your personal intuition for what is right for *you*. Remember to treat yourself well.

It's important that, whatever your age, you look at what you want to achieve and decide what's important to you. Whoever you are, whatever your current circumstances, never underestimate yourself. There can never be another you. The best you is an unstressed you! So relax and remember to respect yourself. As you will see in the chapters ahead, you can create your own particular brand of success that's just right for you.

The more I relax and respect myself, the more confident I become.

NOTES FOR PRACTICAL FOCUS AND RELAXATIONS

Each *Personal Focus* is designed to help you think further about what you've been reading and as a way of applying a self-esteem approach to *your* life, *your* concerns and interests. Space has been left for you to write in. If you want to continue or repeat any *Personal Focus*, just use a notebook.

The relaxations are designed to be used after following the general relaxation procedure. When you are comfortable with this or any other way of relaxing quietly on your own, you can choose an additional relaxation.

PERSONAL FOCUS

Appreciate Yourself

1 Relax and take a breath. Write a list of all the qualities and abilities you like and appreciate about yourself.

If you liked yourself even more, is there something particular you would treat yourself to or something you would do for yourself? Write that down and then do it.

2 Each time you catch yourself being critical, stop and pick up your notepad. Spend a minute or two writing down your good points. If necessary, do this several times a day.

Approve of Yourself

1 Describe a situation where your own self-approval will make all the difference. Maybe you have an interview coming up or a situation where you feel judged, or perhaps you are simply comparing yourself unfavourably to others. How will

you feel when you approve of yourself more? How will added self-approval improve that situation for you?

2 Is there something in your life that you want to do, but you are holding yourself back from by not giving yourself permission? Describe what this is.

Decide to give yourself this permission! What are the things you will now do?

Stop Blaming Yourself

1 Make a list of all those things you constantly blame and berate yourself for.

How do you feel when you read these? Angry or sad? Write that down.

Now ask yourself whether it is helping you in your life to continue to blame yourself. Be quite clear. It's not! Decide you can stop blaming yourself. Have the thought, 'I now choose to stop blaming myself', 'I now choose peace in my life' or any other thoughts you can write down that you know would be helpful in this situation.

What can you do to use your energy to refocus on something joyful, something important to you? Write this out and take action!

Listen to Yourself

Keep a note of hunches, whispers, daydreams about what feels important to you, what you'd love to do. This need only take a few minutes a day. Then look at how you can begin to do some of the things you have recorded. For example, you may not be able to give yourself the holiday of a lifetime right now, yet you can probably take a day off by the sea or an hour off to walk in the park, and meanwhile you can be making plans for that holiday.

Treat Yourself Well

1 List six of the things you know always make *you* feel better, perhaps walking by the river or the sea, relaxing in a bath with aromatherapy oils, massage, talking to a friend, reading, listening to music you love – whatever appeals to *you*. Make one of them something you can do in the next 24 hours.

1
2
3
4
5
6

2 Ask yourself what you could do for yourself today that feels right for you, that feels fun and enjoyable. This is particularly important when you are under pressure and feel you have very little time to yourself. Write it down and do it!

RELAXATIONS

General Relaxation Procedure

Take about ten minutes. Choose a time and place where you can be undisturbed. Sit or lie down comfortably. Take a moment to adjust your body. Gently close your eyes. Really take time to relax your body starting at your head and moving down to your feet. Check that your breathing is relaxed, normal yet relaxed. Let go of any busy thoughts. Just relax, let them go. Don't try to blank your mind, just let go. Pull all your attention back to you; it may be on other people and situations – bring it all back to you.

If you feel your mind full of thoughts then just keep relaxing and letting them go. These are natural reactions, they will pass as you do this relaxation regularly. The same goes for feelings that seem to interfere. Allow them to pass.

When you have finished relaxing and want to get up, just check your body is comfortable, remind yourself that you are relaxed, yet alert, becoming wide awake and full of energy. If you've been lying down, roll over on your side and get up slowly.

Once you are comfortable with the general relaxation, you can add any of the short relaxations. Read through the one that you have chosen before you close your eyes to begin to relax. Pick out the main points. Remember – it's more important to relax than to remember everything that's written down. At the end of the relaxation exercise you can make any notes you want to.

Let Go of Worry

After following the general relaxation given, picture yourself in your mind's eye. Picture yourself taking an empty box of whatever size seems appropriate. This is a very special box that when you put all your worries in, they will be absorbed and dissolved. Just see yourself doing this, off-loading all of those worries, all those ones you never do anything about. Put them in there. Then either walk away from the box, or see it moving away or disappearing. Notice how light and carefree you feel. Gently come out of your relaxation.

Treat Yourself Well

After following the general relaxation given, see yourself in your mind's eye, looking good and feeling good. Let go of any busy thoughts or any upset feelings. Let them go. Put all of your attention on you. As you relax think of all the little things you can do to be nice to yourself to make your day or your week easier and more fun, as well as more fulfilling.

NOTES ON CREATIVE VISUALIZATION

As you follow your practical relaxation procedure you may be able to picture in your mind a relaxing scene or an outcome you'd like to create. Just be sure to include yourself in the picture; notice what you're wearing, doing, the sorts of surroundings you are in. Some of this may present itself to you easily. However, don't worry if the picture doesn't come immediately – just make it up. Remember it's a game and you can send out lines of goodwill so that this picture benefits everyone. Is there anything else to add to the picture? Don't forget to put yourself in the picture! When you feel you have done enough, pause and check that you are relaxed, then gently open your eyes again.

SECTION TWO

Take Control of Your Life

CHAPTER TWO

Your Thoughts as Your Unique Power Base

You are the person who decides, from your point of view, what your day, your life, your world is like. You have all this power because your thoughts, which are yours, are as real as anything you can touch, feel or smell. Now if you let low-level self-esteem thoughts continuously pass through your mind, and most of us do this a lot of the time, for example, 'I'm not doing very well, I'm not good enough, they probably won't like me, I won't be able to, I'm not doing very well, I'm not good enough', then you are going to feel pretty low in energy and not very optimistic. We all know people for whom nothing seems to work, and to hear them talk we begin to understand why – their thoughts are not helpful. They say things like, 'Nothing ever goes right for me.' And it never does! On the other hand there are people whose thoughts are helpful to them. They remember to tell themselves 'I am doing well, I can handle this. Everything is working out for the best!' By doing that, they approach any situation in the best possible way.

A man had set clear goals at work yet never seemed to attain them. He disclosed that all the time he would tell himself that he couldn't do these things and he wasn't good enough, yet the goals he had set himself were not beyond his capabilities. When he changed his thoughts to support himself and continued to take practical action, he achieved what he wanted to do. It is counter-productive to write down goals you want to achieve and at the same time to tell yourself, 'I am not going to be able to do this. It's going to be difficult.' Change those thoughts instead to 'I can do this, it's going smoothly and easily.'

Our thoughts directly affect both how we feel and how we experience our lives. Tell yourself you're hopeless, a failure, enough times and you really will feel and act that way. Tell yourself instead, 'I'm doing well. I'm good enough. People like me, I can do it'. It's easy to see that upgrading our thoughts when we notice they are low will help us to feel better immediately.

I now choose thoughts that help me in my life.

PROGRAMME YOUR MIND IN A HELPFUL WAY

Helpful thoughts help the thinker – that is you; unhelpful thoughts do not. What you think affects how you feel and act. Always remember you have a choice over which thoughts you dwell on. You choose your thoughts. You are who you are very largely because of the thoughts that you have.

Your mind is like a computer. What you programme in you get out. Now when you were very young much of your programme may have been 'written' by parents, teachers and so on. Much of that will have been helpful but some of the thoughts may not be appropriate to adult life as you now live it. Also, children are self-determined beings; at a very early age they form strong opinions and have points of view which may no longer be relevant. You need to make sure that your thoughts are absolutely helpful to you.

You can dissolve or change around thoughts that you want to become true. The important question is not whether or not it is true right now, but whether you want a thought to become true.

It's not appropriate to try to influence other people against their will, particularly in personal matters, yet you can become a sphere of influence by having helpful thoughts. While we cannot directly influence other people, and we certainly cannot *make* them see our point of view, we can certainly affect how we feel about any situation and how we act in it. As well as noticing conscious thoughts that are unhelpful to you, you can become aware of thoughts that are just below the surface, that affect how you behave and feel in various situations. When something recurs or keeps bothering you, it can help to notice if one or more of your underlying thoughts or beliefs is holding you back from achieving the results you say you want. Once you recognize what that thought is, you can dissolve and delete it or change it to a helpful thought.

FOCUS ON THE GOOD IN PEOPLE AND SITUATIONS

You'll find it extremely helpful on a practical level to deliberately focus on helpful, supportive thoughts about a person or a situation. Generosity begins with helpful thoughts about yourself and others. As your self-esteem increases you become more generous in what you want for yourself and others.

You may send out thoughts and feelings of goodwill in advance, for example, towards everyone you work with, telling them in your mind how much you appreciate them and their contribution. Especially in our closest relationships, we tend to put our attention on the bits we don't like, the things we consider aren't working. Instead it can be helpful to deliberately focus on what we do like in a person, what's good about them, their strengths and kindness. Thinking about what is working, what is beneficial, will ensure that you notice and experience more of that.

You'll also feel good when your thoughts are helpful because your thoughts affect you first and more than they affect others. When you have pleasant harmonious thoughts towards other people or about yourself, you feel pleasant and harmonious. When you send out thoughts of hatred and resentment, you're the one who gets the most affected. You receive the curse or blessing of your own thoughts.

What you think won't necessarily affect other people's attitude and behaviour, especially when they have a different 'agenda' from you. There are some people who are not operating from harmony and goodwill and however much you send helpful thoughts they will continue in their own way, so you need to leave them to it and get on with your own life. Happily, there is a tendency, if you put out harmonious thoughts and goodwill to others, to have that returned to you!

My goodwill benefits myself and others.

YOU CHOOSE YOUR THOUGHTS

The most important thing to remember about thoughts is that you choose them. If they are not helpful you can easily change them. A woman who had completed one of our courses reported that when her most unhelpful thoughts about herself came into her mind before an interview, she was able to calmly change them round. She went into the interview situation feeling really good about herself. This ability to choose means that you are never at the mercy of thoughts which are unpleasant and unhelpful either in their affect on you when you're thinking them or in the results. You don't have to entertain those low-level thoughts, you can easily let them go and introduce thoughts that you do want.

I can choose what I think at any moment of my day.

USE YOUR EMOTIONS TO SUPPORT YOUR THOUGHTS

The thoughts we have affect us first, for better or for worse. They may have a great deal of emotion attached to them. This makes them more powerful both in how we're affected by them and in the sort of results we achieve. It is excellent to energize your thoughts with emotional power. However, if you notice that you've moved from a passionate 'I'd love to have this', to a more desperate 'I've *got* to have this', then come back to a more balanced position. A desperate man or woman is not an attractive proposition. From a less desperate and more centred position you are more likely to achieve what you want.

You can go beyond positive thinking to an integrated approach where your mind and emotions are focused on what you want to achieve. If you also connect with your personal intuition to ascertain what is right for you at any time, and then take the appropriate action, you are definitely on course for success.

When you want to have more success in a particular area, you need to identify the helpful thoughts that are right for you. You can change around an old unhelpful thought or introduce a new helpful one, add to this the emotional energy of what you expect to feel when you achieve this goal. Imagine what you will feel like and bring in the feeling right away. This will assist you in drawing to you or achieving the outcome you want.

Both our thoughts and emotions are very powerful. It is when we use them together that we can most help ourselves.

I now choose thoughts that ensure my success.

PERSONAL FOCUS

Choosing Helpful Thoughts

1 Write down all the thoughts about yourself that are supportive and helpful to you. For example, 'I'm a good listener, I get things done'. These are thoughts to remember and to repeat.

2 Write down thoughts that you feel do not help you, for example, 'I'm not good with people, I'll never get this project completed'. When you have identified unhelpful thoughts, dissolve or cancel them. Let them go. You can picture this happening.

3 In a situation that isn't working, notice what you can do from your side to have your thoughts support you and the situation. First write down what you identify as unhelpful thoughts with regard to the situation, for example, 'I'm not good enough to put myself forward for this work; it's taking too long; I'm never going to get this done'.

Now change these to helpful thoughts, for example, 'I'm more than good enough to put myself forward for this work. I complete tasks and projects I've chosen to do with confidence, competence and ease'. Now check at this stage that your adjustments feel right for you. They won't feel immediately true or you wouldn't be bothering to repeat them!

4 If you want success in a particular situation, ask yourself what would be the most helpful thoughts you can hold about the outcome. As well as setting a goal and taking practical action, continually remind yourself of these helpful thoughts for beneficial results. Record and write down your goal for the situation, and the corresponding helpful thought.

RELAXATION

Having Supportive Thoughts

Relaxing in your body and mind, just imagine all unhelpful thoughts dissolving and disappearing. See a lightness and brightness in their place. If there's a situation you are concerned or puzzled about, call in your personal intuition to help identify any unhelpful thoughts so that you can change them round more easily. Now bring in your new helpful thoughts. Imagine yourself in the situation with these new helpful thoughts. Be aware of how good you are feeling. You can bring in this feeling at any time. You know what to do and you will do it. Just gently come out of the relaxation. Now you are ready to take appropriate practical steps.

CHAPTER THREE

Have Your Emotions Help Not Hinder You

Make Friends with Your Feelings

High self-esteem is not about bulldozing over your most sensitive feelings, it is about listening to, respecting and accepting all your emotions, even the ones you wish you didn't have! However, you may find emotions in your life 'difficult'. You are not alone. Many people find that whole area perplexing and even frightening. It seems that although we may be very competent in other ways, for example in our professional lives, when it comes to our emotions we feel very much less sure of ourselves, almost as if we're younger in that area, like a child or adolescent. This problem is not helped by our being expected to put a 'brave face on things' or keep a 'stiff upper lip'.

You may find anger is particularly difficult to handle – whether it's your own or someone else's. Many people do. Very often we learn to hold in our anger and not to show it. You may remember being punished for tantrums as a child or perhaps you've grown up in a family where no one shows their feelings – or just one member does, and do you know when *they* are home! So, of course, you decide that you want none of these emotions. However, the inner grown-up tantrum still goes on!

You may also hold back tears and sadness. While this is

appropriate in a work situation, it is important to be aware of how you are feeling. When you get home you can take some time on your own to cry or be angry if you want to. Let yourself feel the sadness or anger and it will shift and change.

Emotions do change. For example, anger can become determination and sadness can become compassion. It is also more difficult than you think to express pure anger or sadness for long, so you're not going to be stuck with these feelings forever. What is so uncomfortable and exhausting is trying to ward off or keep down your emotions. If you let yourself just gently experience your emotions they will flow on, move and change.

People on programmes often say they're afraid that they'll be overwhelmed by their feelings, that they'll reveal themselves inappropriately at work, or that they will get out of control and cause damage to people or property. On this view of things you would be treating your emotions as the enemy to be fought with or kept down. However, it's by making friends with your feelings that you can best help yourself in moving forward. Our emotions can be a real indication of what we want.

TELLING THE TRUTH TO YOURSELF

Before you decide whether you are going to communicate how you are feeling to another person, you have got to know what that feeling is. You've got to tell the truth to yourself before you can communicate it to another person. You were certainly in touch with your emotions when you were young before you learnt to be 'good' and keep your feelings down or hidden. To help you get back in touch with your feelings on a daily basis, especially when you're uncomfortable with a person or situation, don't ask yourself 'What do I *think* about it?' but ask instead, 'What do I really *feel* about this person or situation?' When you recognize your body is full of anger it's good to release it by, for example, having a brisk

walk, going for a jog, or whatever means of physical move-
ment is appropriate. However, while this will help tem-
porarily, nothing will change or shift long term until we
release the emotional component and change our mental
patterns at the level of our thoughts. When you've been
putting other people's feelings before your own and subsequently most likely feeling resentful, then for a period of
two weeks ask yourself about any situation, 'Is this best for
me?' You may be surprised by your answers!

I now listen to and respect what I am feeling.

WHEN YOU FEEL HURT LET GO OF BLAME

When you're angry and upset with another person it pulls
you off course perhaps more than anything else. Our deepest
feelings are prompted by those with whom we have an
intimate relationship or see daily at work. You'll feel bad and
also find it a very difficult situation to cope with. Even when
you are not physically in that person's presence you will find
a lot of time is taken up in thinking about him or her.

Sometimes you feel so mad with someone you feel you
could kill them. You may pretend there is nothing wrong
between you, that you don't care and are neutral. You never
are! It's better to tell the truth to yourself when any of your
relationships are out of harmony. We always know when
we're troubled by a relationship with another person. Emotional turmoil will often accompany our thinking, as we go
over and over the situation and how unfair it is. They may
be the last person we want to think of, but they will be the
first person on our mind! Our thoughts and emotions will
feel totally tied up with them. If the difficulty is with someone at work you may vow that you're not going to bother
with that person until the next day. Yet who is on your mind
the moment you leave work? Who is on your mind most of
the evening? Isn't it that person?

When you're going through upset it's important to realize within yourself how you are feeling, whether it's anger, sadness, fear or jealousy. As you gently relax and breathe deeply you can begin to let your emotions move. Our emotions are always changing and you will feel differently soon. You can help yourself by relaxing and feeling your feelings. It doesn't help to pretend to ourselves that we're not feeling these emotions. When we keep pushing them down we become exhausted and even ill. You may also be thinking of how you can hurt the person you feel has hurt you. That is a natural first reaction. You may plot your revenge, imagining that will make you feel better, and you may say you only want to see justice done. At this point, peace of mind seems as though it doesn't feature. The angry resentful thoughts you have are making you feel even worse. Your thoughts and your time and energy get caught up. So what can you do?

If you really want to move through this, you need to be willing to have a change of heart, for even if you are never going to see the person or people concerned again, these binding ties of blame will weigh *you* down unless you resolve them. It can be particularly difficult to let go of resentment when everyone agrees you are in the right. It can help you to remember times when you yourself have been less than loving, helpful or considerate to another person. When you think about those times you'll realize you didn't feel too good about yourself; perhaps you were worried about something, not getting along with someone you're close to, or generally suffering a loss of confidence. When we are only just coping we may sometimes act totally inappropriately or even cruelly, especially when underneath it all we are really quite scared. It may help you to consider this, for the same may apply to the person who has treated you so badly. However, as a general rule of thumb you can know that the more obnoxious a person is being or has been, the more screwed up he or she is. This is especially true when people are presenting a cold, uncaring, impassive front.

The only way to regain peace of mind, and it may feel like your sanity, is to be willing to set yourself free by getting these offences out of your heart. As you begin to do this you'll start to be released, and as you continue you'll find you let go more and more each day, feeling better and better as you do so.

I now let myself feel peaceful.

RECOGNIZE WHICH FEELINGS ARE YOURS

Notice how you are affected by other people's feelings and emotions; you almost seem to pick up their anger or sadness. This happens frequently to young children who are very 'absorbent' of other people's emotions. Consciously remind yourself that these are not your feelings and then you can let them go. Let go of that negative energy. Take a walk around the block. Focus back on yourself and what you need to be doing.

It's important to recognize what *you* are feeling, and either enjoy those feelings or relax and allow them to change or move. The more you integrate your disturbing feelings, rather than suppressing them, the better you will feel about yourself and the more focused you will be on accomplishing what is important to you.

We all have times when we feel we have got off track, wasted time, energy and money. This can be particularly upsetting if we've been longing to do something and feel we have let ourselves get distracted and caught up in problems which are other people's and not our own. If this happens to you, vigorously pull back your attention from concerns with other people, areas that you do not want to give time and energy to, and place this energy on your own hopes and dreams. It's difficult when you feel you've experienced injustice and want to redress that, or you want to protect and defend yourself, yet see if you can do this without allowing the people or situation to claim any more of your energy. Let go of blaming yourself for having spent so much time, energy or money on the situation.

It's easy with hindsight to see we could have acted differently and just got on with what was important to us, yet we are always doing the best we can at any time. There is no doubt that there are destructive people, unpleasant people, who maliciously try to upset or cause hurt to others. While we may know they are disturbed, it doesn't making dealing with them any less time-consuming. So if you get caught up in a situation like that, follow through to protect your rights, yet pull back on the emotional level. Acknowledge to yourself how angry you feel at not having done things differently, and then let go. Just let go and proceed with what is important to you.

I now let go of emotions I don't want.

DIMINISH FEAR AND PANIC

When you're feeling frightened of what may happen in the future, of a particular event or encounter that you dread, or you are panicking about a situation, it is possible to reclaim your self-esteem and feel centred again. First you need to relax your body and to let yourself feel the fear. As you do this it will begin to move through you. Bring in a feeling of courage to help dispel your fear. Then remind yourself that you are safe, that you can handle the situation or person involved. Now work out what you need to do for the outcome you want, what steps you need to take, perhaps what you need to say. Decide if this is something that you want to do right now and be honest. If it's going to take a lot of your time and energy and you're involved in an important project, you may choose to postpone it, but check you are not doing so out of fear. Seek out those people who will support you in moving forward with this. Then take the first step. As you take action you will experience less fear.

Looking After Yourself

In times of emotional crisis nurture yourself and look after yourself, see that your physical needs are met with attention to nutritious food, moderate exercise, fresh air, and relaxation. Also talk to friends and family who love and support you. Decide what it would be joyful for you to do and also what you can do that is important and will assist you in your purpose. Put in place the steps you have decided. You can envisage a joyful future full of all you can wish for yourself. Feel comforted in the middle of apparent tests and trials. When it feels as though calamity has struck, relax and follow your own guidance. Consciously postpone making a decision if that is what is necessary. Stay centred and don't get sucked into who is to blame. Do what is best for yourself, keeping happy. Do what needs to be done, if anything, to rectify the situation. Put your attention on what's important to you. Have around you supportive friends who will both acknowledge your feelings and gently remind you to have supportive thoughts.

You Choose How You Feel

It comes as a surprise to some people to hear they can choose and change their emotions. It is not helpful to just hope you'll feel better soon or to try and snap out of your depressed feelings. Trying to push away feelings you don't want and to cling desperately to feelings you do want doesn't work either. When you let yourself feel your feelings they flow and change rather than staying stuck. When there's no prospect of much to do that's appealing, you can feel quite low and gloomy. However, if you suddenly get an invitation to do something exciting later in the day, notice how your emotions immediately change. You feel uplifted and enthusiastic again. This shows how quickly your emotions can shift.

Now there won't always be an exciting offer from someone else at a time when you're feeling low. What is important is to learn to prompt that change of feeling within yourself by introducing helpful thoughts and imagining a more exciting or delightful outcome. You can also bring in happier feelings by remembering pleasant past experiences.

Changing round thoughts that don't help you can actually change how you're feeling. If you're particularly low, write out your unhelpful thoughts. No wonder you feel low – anyone having those thoughts would! Now rewrite those thoughts so that they are more supportive. You'll definitely feel better. Then you can keep repeating this process until you feel good again. Try this, especially if you don't feel like it – you'll be surprised how well it works!

NO ONE ELSE CAN MAKE YOU HAPPY

An important part of self-esteem is realizing that no-one else can make you happy. You are independent and responsible for yourself. As well as having an interdependence with other people, you are responsible for your own well-being and happiness. The good news is that when you follow your personal intuition you will automatically do what is best and necessary for you with regard to your work, health, relationships with others and your home. This will include, for example, going to appropriate health practitioners or getting the advice you want with regard to an aspect of your work.

The tendency we have is to assume that someone else will make us feel better physically, mentally or emotionally. The truth is that we must take the lead ourselves. Although advice and information from others is important, only you can know what is best for you and whether the advice from others is right for you, as an individual unique person.

While you need to identify thoughts and attitudes that don't support your self-esteem or your life, while you need to recognize your feelings in order to let them flow through, it is never helpful for you to dwell on angry, or sad thoughts and feelings, for they cover you like a shroud and inhibit your progress and sense of self-worth. Once you make a decision to be happy you can then help yourself in all sorts of ways, by not getting over-tired, having a balance of activity and relaxation, with support from others.

Most of all you can support yourself in how you think of yourself and others, practising self-respect, respect for others, letting go of blaming yourself and others. For we feel happiness when we act in accordance with our personal intuition of what is right and appropriate, when we behave responsibly and honestly. As you know yourself better, you become aware of your choices. Decisions you make out of love and wanting to grow lead to happiness. Your happiness relates to your purpose, your sense of having something worthwhile to do and contribute. You then trust not in fate or external destiny but in the results of your own right thoughts and action.

I now decide to be happy.

PERSONAL FOCUS

Have Your Emotions Help You

1   For the next two weeks, when you feel uneasy or uncomfortable just ask yourself 'What do I feel about this?' When you've been putting everyone first, ask of different situations 'What is best for *me*?' Record some of your responses.

2   Write down emotions that you want to feel. What do you want to have as your focus? By noticing that and reminding yourself of them, the emotional emphasis you experience will shift.

3 Be aware of and write down how your emotions change when you're with particular people. For example, spending time with someone who is very negative will tend to drag you down. On the other hand, when you're feeling low, someone enthusiastic and encouraging will give you a boost. Record that as a guide to your understanding.

4 Notice which emotions are yours and which are another person's. Then consciously let go of the emotions which are not yours. This will be helpful in maintaining clarity and harmony.

Free Yourself from Blaming

If you think that you don't want to waste this exercise on a certain person, that is probably the very person to use it on! You may want to re-read the sections on When You Feel Hurt (page 30) and Recognize Which Feelings are Yours (page 32) before doing this exercise. There may be more than one person that you think of, in which case start with the first person that comes to mind.

1 Write down the name of the person, you feel upset with or hurt by.

2 List all the things you blame them for, all you feel hurt or affected by.

3 As you write this out, how are you feeling?

Do you want revenge or do you want to be free and happy? If the latter, then decide to stop blaming. Continue to remind yourself of this when you next think of the person, and your upset will diminish and hurt feelings dissolve.

4 Determinedly pull your attention back to yourself. Focus on what you want to achieve. What can you do that is important to you? What can you do that is joyful for you?

When You Feel Upset

1 Write down how you're feeling.

2 What action can you take for yourself that will repair the hurt feelings you've been experiencing? Write this down.

3 Write out your most supportive thoughts for yourself at the moment.

4 Even if you have to force yourself, notice what you need to focus on. What is important to you? What can you do that will help you to feel better?

RELAXATION

Moving into Greater Success

Get into your relaxed state of comfort and confidence. See and feel yourself looking great and feeling good, calm yet enthusiastic, full of life. Notice all you have already working for you, how rich your life is right now and for the future. See your anger towards a particular person shaking out like little arrows out of you, so it dissolves into nothing. As you're the best person to spend your energy on now, see yourself moving forward, supercharged with your own energy. Imagine all the force of the wrong committed against you now propelling you forward with magnified intensity.

You go into greater and greater success and happiness. Now relax totally. Take a moment before you gently open your eyes.

CHAPTER FOUR

Your Personal Intuition

LISTEN TO YOURSELF

When situations or circumstances seem to be trying or difficult, we often wonder what to do for the best. Sometimes we go all round the houses, literally, in an attempt to work out what to do. The truth is that the answers to what we need and want to know lie within each of us and can be obtained by listening to our personal intuition. There will be times when you require, for example, more information or advice on legal procedures, yet with regard to the sorts of questions you most constantly ask yourself – eg 'What should I do next with regard to this?', 'How do I really want to relate to this person?', or 'What is the right thing for me to do here?' – the answers lie within you. However, although you keep saying, 'I wish I knew what to do', you may be so busy, so frantic, so stressed that you never really wait to hear any answers from your personal intuition.

Your personal intuition is a vital part of your self-esteem. It guides you in doing what is best for you as a unique individual human being. What is best for another person may not necessarily be best for you. Your personal intuition is an inner voice that guides you, makes you special and your life precious. Without your personal intuition, much energy will be wasted, it is like moving along a road with no clear idea of where you are going and with no light to guide you. To begin with you may feel most in touch with your personal intuition when you have your relaxation time, when your mind and body begin to feel calmer and more relaxed. After a few weeks, as you practise pausing and relaxing, you can get more in touch with your intuition throughout the day.

As I listen to my personal intuition I know what's right for me.

RECOGNIZING YOUR PERSONAL INTUITION

You may have had the experience of following through successfully on a hunch. You may have also experienced your personal intuition when you have given up trying to work out a problem, done something else and the solution has presented itself. However, this can be a hit-or-miss way of working things out and can also take a long time. Finding a way to do this systematically and regularly will bring you more of the results and answers you want. While you are tensing your body and your mind, it is more difficult to listen to your personal intuition. So learning to relax your body and let go of busy thoughts is very practical. When you do this regularly you will feel calmer and more centred. You become aware of the answers to personal questions that you have been perplexed about for some time. Most of us need to get into the habit of relaxing and getting calm first.

Your personal intuition is always compassionate to yourself and others. It will not suggest you go further forward with another person or an endeavour than is appropriate for you at any time. Using your personal intuition you will feel a sense of 'this is right for me' when you carry it out. You will also feel comfortable in your body. Although it can sometimes seem an unusual step that your personal intuition suggests, often it's very practical.

MAKE THE BEST USE OF YOUR TIME

Once you learn to begin to relax your body and mind it gets easier and easier to listen, to become aware of what is appropriate for you. You may not at first recognize the answer, or you may get it at another time. At different times throughout the day, in the middle of your activities you can learn to centre yourself and ask yourself 'What is it best that I do next?' or realign when you seem to be off track or wasting time. Listening to your intuition is a marvellous time-management tool. Your personal intuition is the key to what is right for you, as a unique individual, at any time.

The more I listen to my personal intuition the better I manage my personal time and energy.

YOU CAN TRUST YOURSELF

You can ask yourself what you want to know and listen to your answers. You won't usually get detailed answers for years ahead – that would not be in keeping with the way life evolves, changes and flows. You will, however, be aware of enough for you to trust that you are always going to know how to behave and act. You will realize what the appropriate steps are for you to take at any time. Sometimes your advice to yourself will be to wait and not take action.

When you listen to your intuition and act appropriately it will protect you from doing things that are not respectful towards yourself and others. It can stop you from saying 'Yes' when you want to say 'No' and saying 'No' when you want to say 'Yes'. Your personal intuition will put you in touch with your purpose for life and what is important to you. This will gradually unfold.

When you first start to listen to your personal intuition you may wonder, 'Is that my fear speaking, or even prejudice?' It's helpful to distinguish your personal intuition from fear by asking yourself 'What would I do if I didn't feel so afraid?' However, there is no need to push yourself beyond what feels appropriate for you. You're always going to feel some fear anyway, so you just need to move forward with what you want to do.

I always trust myself to know what to say and do.

DEVELOPING YOUR PERSONAL INTUITION

You develop your personal intuition by identifying it and most importantly by using it. You will already have experienced your personal intuition in hunches, in knowing who is calling you when the phone goes, or thinking of a friend and finding out they were thinking of you. Learn to be quiet and listen to your personal intuition on a daily basis and you will establish that link, making it easier to help yourself when you feel a situation is very urgent and important.

Our intuition is for our personal use, so take care when using your intuition about what other people 'should' do. Also, when someone wants an explanation – especially when you know your motives may be suspect or not fully thought out – just saying it was your intuition won't do!

GOAL-SETTING

It is important to set goals using your personal intuition. When you do this the goals you set will be appropriate for you and you can take practical steps with a better sense of right timing. Although it is good to have clear and precise goals, it is also important to leave some leeway over how these goals may come to you. You need both long-term and short-term goals. Be focused yet flexible. You'll discover new ways of doing things and a greater creativity. At work, it can lead to new products and services. Used in a systematic way at work your personal intuition increases your productivity and efficiency. There is greater harmony in a group, family or a team when people are operating from their personal intuition rather than from their ego. Using your personal intuition is better for you and others.

THE KEY TO YOUR INNER PATTERN

Just as seeds grow into flowers and fruit, we all have within us an inner pattern or blueprint for perfection. By its nature this pattern is unique, special to each individual. One person's unique blueprint will never be right for another person to follow. We will naturally feel more joyful and fulfilled when we follow what is the perfect outworking of our inner pattern. How do we get in touch and know what this inner pattern is? Obviously, because each person is unique and special, no one else can tell us what it is. The key to this understanding of yourself is listening to your personal intuition.

Often our recurring daydreams can provide clues, particularly where we see ourselves carrying out work which we would love, or acting in a way which is helpful to and serves others. What are your recurring daydreams? Do they not contain the seeds of what at your best you can be, what you would love to be doing?

Sometimes we see another person doing something and, while no one person can truly emulate another, we know we'd love to do that or something similar. Trust that inner sense of knowing. We can come back also to ourselves and our inner pattern in our quiet times, particularly with regard to our sense of direction or purpose. We can ask questions that will help our blueprint to unfold, bearing in mind that aspects of it will be chosen by us. We can ask ourselves 'What is it really important for me to do?', 'How do I want to live my life?', 'What do I truly want to achieve?' The answers will come, perhaps gradually, requiring us to keep a notebook handy and to take action as appropriate.

You will begin to notice that there are certain activities

which for you are more energizing. Begin to imagine what the perfect life, the perfect work, would be for you. You can write out and describe this. However, you do need to make this finding out, this unfolding of your inner blueprint and sense of direction, important for you, a priority. Establish the habit of listening to your personal intuition when you relax each day, then at other times of the day it will become easier to pause and touch base with yourself. When you have a certainty of your direction and purpose, so much else falls into perspective.

PERSONAL FOCUS AND RELAXATIONS

Listening to Your Personal Intuition

Get yourself *fully relaxed* and then gently open your eyes. Stay relaxed as you complete the following.

1 Look at how you plan to spend tomorrow and consider if this is spending time in the most valuable way for you. Make any adjustments you can in line with your self-esteem and personal intuition.

2 In your notebook keep a record of your daydreams and of anything that gives you joy or a surge of energy. Do any of your practical plans give you this same surge of energy and excitement? These are the plans to develop.

3 Write below two questions that you would like to have answers to. Get yourself in a relaxed state, perhaps with music, and then listen to your personal intuition. Suggestions may come at this time or later. As you become alert again you can assess what you want to do about this information, and take appropriate practical steps.

Goal-Setting

1 Specific steps are extremely helpful in goal-setting and you need to write them down. You probably do that when you go to the supermarket, so please do that for your life! From a relaxed position, feeling in touch with your personal intuition, look at the goals you want for your life. Clarify these in as much detail as you can.

2 Outline and write down specific goals over a number of set time-frames chosen by you. Where will you be with this goal in a year or six months? Now draw it nearer. Where do you want to be in a month or two? However long-term your goals may be, you still need the regular achievement of short-term goals.

3 Given your goal (in 2 above), write down those self-esteem thoughts that will be most helpful to you, and then, on the next line, write down any people who will support you in achieving that goal. Below that, list those practical steps you need to take.

CHAPTER FIVE

Managing Stress, Change and Your Time

RECOGNIZE WHEN YOU ARE STRESSED

Although the symptoms of stress are well-documented, you will have a unique response to stress. You may, for example, feel physically unwell or be emotionally upset, unable to relax and exhausted. Perhaps you feel unable to think straight and that your energies are scattered. You may become upset by 'small' things and be anxious and snappy in your interactions with other people. It is likely you will make decisions that are not in your best interest because you do not pause to listen to yourself, to your personal intuition – those hunches that guide you as to what it is best for you to do.

THE CAUSES OF STRESS

When we look at what causes stress, it may seem that we suffer when we have too much to do or try to do too much in too short a space of time. We may feel rushed into making decisions before we are ready. But are you aware that the biggest stressor of all is low self-esteem? When you consider the way you think about yourself and others when you are under pressure, you can understand why this is so, for when things are difficult your most unhelpful thoughts surface. For example, as soon as you tell yourself 'I am not of much value', 'I'll never get this done', your stress level rises. In other words, it is not the actual events but the thoughts we have about them that cause us most stress. If we tell ourselves, for example, how well we are doing and how much we are achieving considering the circumstances, instead of focusing on how badly we are doing and how slowly we are progressing, we will immediately reduce stress levels. Now that you know how to raise the level of your self-esteem you can start to reduce the level of stress in your life.

As I raise my self-esteem I reduce stress in my life.

Another cause of stress is not having identified a purpose for yourself. This is when you don't know what to do with your talents and abilities, whether in your work or leisure time. Without this direction for your energy it can be stressful for you and those around you as you will tend to want other people to make you feel fulfilled instead of doing this for yourself. There is also a tendency to blame other people rather than listening to yourself as to what is appropriate for you.

Having to work with a difficult person or people is very stressful. We can feel we have no control of the situation and that we are unable to change. Though inappropriate behaviour can sometimes be checked at work, it is very often someone's manner rather than actual misconduct that is so distressing. While you can and should ask for what you want, you need to work on the basis that the other person may not change. Your tactics here are to reduce your stress and discomfort, and to stop wasting your energy on them. Respect yourself by standing up for yourself, pull back your emotional energy and focus on yourself. Where you feel a lack of respect and appreciation from, for example, your boss, remind yourself of your helpful thoughts. For example, 'I am doing a good job', 'I appreciate and approve of myself', 'My contribution is of great value'. By choosing these helpful thoughts when you feel under pressure or unappreciated, you lower the level of stress and raise the level of your self-esteem.

Much of what we call stress is fear and worry – worry over the past or fear of the future. You can choose to think differently about the past, and your helpful thoughts and actions in the present are the best insurance of future success. One of the constants in life is change and with this comes uncertainty. It isn't appropriate for us to know exactly what is going to happen. We are in a world of constantly changing possibilities and opportunities. Although you may not have the security of knowing certain outcomes, there is no need to experience stress, distress or fear. Have the self-esteem to be aware that you can depend on yourself to know what to do for the best at any time. This builds up your inner security so that you will be able to cope with and make the best of any situation.

My real security comes from me.

Lifestyle Balance

Particularly in times of stress and rapid change where it can happen that at least one area of our lives, be it work or a relationship, changes overnight, it can help us if we already have balance in our lives.

Sometimes you may need to spend a great deal of time and energy on work, while at other times you feel the need to get back in touch with friends or arrange to spend time with your family. Whatever your major commitments, it's important to pay some attention to the other areas and particularly to look after your health and appearance. Most important of all, make time and space to do what is joyful for you, even if the time you spend is relatively short. This is vital for your self-esteem and will give you more energy and enthusiasm for the parts of life which seem perhaps like a duty right now.

Regular relaxation will help you feel calmer. It is vital at all times to have some peace and quiet where you can listen to your personal intuition and see things from a balanced perspective.

A manager who was feeling very stressed at work, with a lot of duties to attend to and decisions to make, felt he couldn't take the time to relax. However, things got so bad that as a last resort he was willing to try setting aside time to relax. He was amazed at what a difference it made. Not only could he see more clearly what he had to do, but many more opportunities and possibilities presented themselves. He decided that relaxing and listening to himself was the best time-management aid he had come across!

As you relax more and develop a way of thinking that is helpful, you can more easily keep focused and identify more clearly the practical steps you need to take.

I create harmony in my life.

YOU CAN HANDLE CHANGE

Nowadays many things are changing, nothing seems to stay the same. It can feel very frightening when what you took for granted becomes uncertain: jobs that we thought were for life suddenly disappear, relationships we assumed would last forever break up. We've placed so much importance on external structures that when they fall apart or when people don't live up to our expectations we feel lost.

While we can do our part, we can't change other people. If our well-being and happiness depend on everything that we want happening when we want it, and other people's falling in line with us, we will be continually frustrated. This is particularly so when the people involved are part of a large organization with its own priorities or part of a large family. This should not stop you being clear about what you want.

If you are initiating the changes, use your personal intuition to clarify and define exactly what you want. Write out your goals to ensure that your thoughts are helpful, then be prepared to take appropriate action, which may mean persevering until you achieve the changes you want. As appropriate, you can take steps to keep your stress levels down and check that your life remains in balance. This is energizing and will assist you in making the changes you want.

If your changes affect other people, remember they will feel better if they are involved in the process of change. Where changes are unwanted, for example at work, you can help other people by being calm and reassuring. While being truthful, focus on the opportunities for individuals that the change will offer.

YOU WILL COME THROUGH CRISIS

You are likely to feel out of control and fearful when changes in your circumstances are ongoing; when they are unexpected and undesired you experience a crisis situation. Perhaps your job or an important relationship that you had imagined were secure turn out not to be. You're not only coping with a situation not of your choosing and which you do not want, but you're having to let go of something that you did want, that you loved. All this is shocking to you and will affect you in different ways. Feeling as though you are in a crisis is not at all unusual today. It is an experience that many of you may be going through or have gone through. The emphasis is on *going through*. You may not feel that you will make it, but you will come through it.

It is therefore important to acknowledge that you have these feelings. Set aside a time on your own to allow yourself to feel your anger and sadness. You can also do something physical, like a brisk walk, a swim or a game of tennis. This will help to calm your emotions by releasing that pent-up physical tension. You will also need to move through whatever is causing you pain, which means letting go of blaming. Dealing with emotions on a daily basis can help you integrate them.

When you are moving through a time of emotional upset,

it's important to be aware you may be distracted as your mind constantly returns to the problem. So take care to avoid any minor mishaps when you are boiling kettles or crossing the road. Notice where you are putting things so you don't lose tickets, documents, and so on. A little extra attention is needed at this time. Take special care of yourself for a while.

Look after yourself and accept support in a crisis. Physically you may feel awful – unable to sleep, sick, unable to relax. Because you are suffering from shock, your mind may be all over the place, trying to work out what is going on, what went wrong. You may be feeling emotional pain with seemingly no way of resolving or accepting the situation. Acknowledge that you need comforting now and let friends and family be supportive. Ask for support, work out a way forward. Within you, you have the quality of courage. Allow it to come through to assist you.

I stay centred even when things change.

USE CHANGE AND CRISIS TO CREATE OPPORTUNITIES

The key word for a time of crisis is focus. Focus and refocus on what is important to you. Each day look at what you can do that will bring you joy. It may be simple, like going for a walk, talking to a supportive friend on the phone, having a relaxing bath – do it! Also, determinedly, courageously, focus on what is really important, what is in line with your purpose. Listen to your personal intuition and follow it.

As you regain your self-esteem, re-experience your self-value and diminish your fear, you can begin to notice the opportunities that lie even within your current situation. When we feel changes being thrust upon us we can be very resistant. Certainly we need to take steps to ensure that we're not being forced into doing something that isn't in our best interests, but it's always helpful to look for any opportunities this change may bring.

Although it may seem unlikely at first, be open to the possibility that the change could lead to things getting better rather than getting worse, that you may end up with far more than you had previously. For example, you may have been made redundant but you perhaps no longer have to do a job that you hate. You may be having difficulty over your rights as an individual, as a consumer, a tenant, an employee at the moment. However, you could end up with greater rights than previously. From this acknowledgement of potential, begin to look at how you would want things to work out. What do you really want for yourself with regard to, for example, the work you want to do, the way you want to be treated? Start to picture this in your mind. How can you create opportunities? Introduce helpful thoughts and start to relax and listen to your personal intuition.

Changes can be very much for the better, all sorts of new and exciting possibilities can open up for us – new people, new and better ways of doing things, with greater happiness and greater fulfilment. You may be able to recall changes you felt forced into and later realized were for the best. For example, a woman was forced to move out of a work situation by her business partner. Although it was initially very unpleasant and she felt there was nothing she could do, it became a spur to her to set up her own successful PR company.

From a point of high self-esteem, focus on the best possible outcome, one that brings you joy and is in line with your purpose; look for immediate as well as long-term advantages. Relax and notice what steps suggest themselves to you that you can put into practice right away.

I focus on and recognize opportunities.

YOU CAN CREATE MORE TIME

Are you having the time of your life, or feeling you haven't the time to live your life? Do you complain you never have enough time. This seems to be very much a part of the way we live our lives nowadays and almost everyone feels stressed and under pressure. How often do you hear people say, or say to yourself, 'I never have enough time'? The more you focus on and repeat this the more true it becomes for you. Often we get tense, panic, and achieve far less than we would do if we went about things calmly and in a relaxed way. So begin telling yourself that you do have enough time!

Even within a busy job we don't ask ourselves what we want to achieve. Many time management systems simply don't work because people are out of touch with their own personal intuition as to what would be best for them to do at any time. Use feelings of shortage of time to help you prioritize. Look again at how you can organize your time so you can complete your priorities and recognize that these priorities may change. As you listen to your personal intuition very often short cuts, better ways of achieving things, emerge. Even a short time spent quietly on your own, whether in the business setting or at home, can save you much struggle, frustration, time and money. You can use your personal intuition for an overview of the situation or task and work out what practical steps to take.

You may say, 'How can I be relaxed and calm when there's so much to do?' When you stop for a moment, you'll realize that you achieve a lot less by panicking and being tense. Sometimes taking a break is just what is needed and wanted. You'll also know that when you're absorbed in something you love which captures your imagination, you don't think about time; sometimes hours go by without your realizing, or you seem to achieve a great deal in a surprisingly short time. If you panic when you're with people at work or at home, everybody becomes tense and edgy. Less gets done, more mistakes are made and a good deal of illfeeling is generated. Should you be in this situation then calm down and centre yourself; not only will you achieve more but the whole atmosphere will improve.

Think about the times when you've attended to things which seemed urgent to someone else, or times when you've chatted to colleagues or friends when you had something else you really wanted to complete either at home or at work. Compare this to the times when you've known the most important thing you've wanted to do or achieve, focused on that and completed it, not allowing yourself to become distracted. You'll be aware how satisfying that is.

Because you are special, a unique being with your own requirements and desires, using your time well will depend on using your personal intuition to identify what is important for you to do. Just think: if you spent your time on what was best for you, everything would change for the better very quickly. You can create this for yourself by listening to your personal intuition before you set goals for yourself and act.

As I relax and centre myself I achieve more.

PERSONAL FOCUS

Controlling Stress

1 Spend a few minutes, at least every other day, consciously relaxing. It can be helpful to fit in a quiet time on your own every day, even for a few minutes. Make a note of the date and time of your relaxations and quiet times so that you can monitor any reduction in your stress level.

2 Get your emotions out of your system! Write down your feelings and then let go of blaming yourself and other people so that you can use all of your available energy for you to move forward with self-esteem. Physical exercise can help integrate uncomfortable feelings.

3 Although you may have spoken to various people about your situation, see if you can write it out without emotion, viewing it objectively as a situation rather than an upsetting crisis.

4 Relax and listen to your personal intuition. Be aware of any hunches about what steps you need to take to improve the situation that is particularly stressful for you. If you have been distracted, now put your whole attention on what is important to you. This will begin to lift you, raising your self-esteem and your energy level.

Lifestyle Balance

1 Notice the overall balance in your life, whether for example, the various areas such as home, friends, work, garden or time for yourself are as you would like them to be. Write out any improvements or additions you want to make.

2 Look at one practical step you will need to take in each area. Write down what these are and when you will do them.

3 When you want to focus in more detail on one area of your life, write out your goals for a set time-frame, perhaps the next year. Then break these down into medium-term goals of, say, six months, shorter-term goals of three months, and also your aims for the next month. Write down and put in place the practical steps you need to take and include your most helpful self-esteem thoughts.

Managing Change

1 Using your personal intuition, outline the change you want or need to make, then write it out as a goal.

2 Describe your feelings about making this change, eg fear or excitement.

3 What is your most helpful thought about this situation?

4 Who will support you through this change and who will benefit from your support?

5 If this is a major on-going change, how will you deal with the stress and keep your life-style in balance? Make your notes here.

6 Using your personal intuition, outline the steps you need to take.

Coping with Change to Create Opportunity

Do this exercise from a relaxed perspective listening to your personal intuition.

1 Can you find any helpful aspects to a situation of change, any ways it is benefiting you? Write them here.

2 Is there a way you could use the situation to create opportunities for yourself. What steps can you take? Record them here and see when you might do them.

3 As you relax, see if you can bring to mind an overview of the situation noticing if there is anything else that it would help you to know or to do. Be aware that the answer will either come now or later.

The Best Use of Your Time

First get in a relaxed state and be open to any insights from your personal intuition on what you want to achieve.

1 When making plans, look at what you want to achieve long-term and short-term, breaking this down into manageable steps. Build in flexibility as to the order in which you may act, and review your priorities from time to time.

2 With regard to what you are planning to do tomorrow, relax, get in touch with your personal intuition, and decide if that is in fact the best use of your time. Are you doing what is important for you? Make any adjustments necessary.

RELAXATIONS

Let Go of Stress

Get in a relaxed and comfortable position. Imagine and picture all of the stress and tension leaving your body and dissolving so that your energy is now calm and smooth. Picture yourself looking calm, centred and revitalized. Remind yourself you are strong enough to handle any challenge. Listen to your personal intuition with regard to what it would help you to do. Be open to any answers as you listen to yourself, to your personal intuition. You may hear these now or later. Write them down.

Change and Opportunity

After the general relaxation procedure, relax a little more and see yourself in your mind's eye looking good and feeling confident. Envisage the change that you would like or see yourself easily handling a change that you are faced with. Picture yourself taking the steps to move through this to a beneficial outcome. Relax a little longer – daydream – imagine a wonderful outcome. Take your time. When you are ready, gently open your eyes and write down any ideas you had while relaxing in this way.

SECTION THREE

Your Individuality

CHAPTER SIX

Recognize Your Individuality

BELIEVE IN YOURSELF

You will probably have already suspected that you can be your own best friend or your own worst enemy. More precisely, your biggest enemy is self-doubt, your greatest friend is self-belief. Can you believe the best of yourself – that you are capable of giving your best and that you deserve to receive the best? Do you believe that you can do what is important to you?

The decisive factor in whether you will or can achieve something is your belief in yourself. On one of our programmes there was a man who knew that he had the talent and skills to do a more fulfilling job than he was doing, yet at interviews he would get 'Thank you, but no thank you' or 'Great, but not this time'! That was until he really stepped up his own belief in himself. This was not just an outer appearance of confidence but a real inner belief which led to work he really wanted.

Do you believe in yourself enough to do what you want to do? If you really want to achieve something, as well as taking the practical steps you must reach a point of sustained belief in yourself, instead of expecting the worst and as a result feeling very fearful. Stop criticizing yourself and, where you can, be gentle with yourself. Let go of worried, stressful thoughts. You are a unique individual person. What is right for someone else will not necessarily be right for you. So listen to yourself, as well as telling yourself helpful thoughts during the day and taking practical action. This will aid you in sustaining your self-belief.

I believe in myself.

Whatever the situation or circumstances you as an individual find yourself in right now, start with self-value. It may be that you need to value yourself more to progress with the work you want to do. It may be that a relationship you had thought was a lasting one has changed, or a job you felt was secure has gone. This does not mean to say that you are not still of great value: you are. It is easy to feel hopeless and discouraged in such circumstances, yet that does not help. To move beyond this, you need to feel a sense of self-value that is there unconditionally. This self-value can only be added by you. No other person can do this for you.

Deliberately valuing yourself in this way is appropriate, especially where you feel a lack of self-value is holding you back or that greater self-value would assist you in moving forward. This may be in doing more of what is really appropriate for you or in asking for the additional money you know you deserve for the work you do. Realize how worthwhile and valuable you are. You have many unique qualities, many good aspects and abilities. You will have developed helpful characteristics and learned much. It is important to remember and hold on to the fact that all of these aspects which constitute your self-value are always there. In fact, they may even have been added to by adversity. Challenging circumstances make you more, not less.

I value myself at all times.

BEING THE BEST YOU

It's never too late nor too early to be the person you want to be! However, you need to prepare and set up the conditions to allow that to happen. This will involve changing your thoughts and attitudes. It may mean, for example, learning to make presentations and overcoming your fear of speaking in public. Because a large part of expressing your uniqueness will be through the work you choose to do, you may need to train, to learn and to gain the necessary experience.

In any area of your life where you want changes or improvements, you need to change your inner beliefs about yourself and what is possible. This will change your self-image as you project it to others. You will also need to take certain practical steps. These may be prompted by your personal intuition as being appropriate. At first, they will feel deliberate rather than 'natural' yet they will prove to be appropriate actions for the changes you want to bring about.

Deciding you are going to be more of the person you want to be does mean letting go of old habits, old ways of thinking, particularly about yourself. When you catch yourself being unhelpful with regard to the way you are thinking about yourself, then change your thinking. Bring in more helpful thoughts, telling yourself that you can accomplish some-thing, you know what you want, that a positive outcome is being reached. When you are feeling confident it's easier to take appropriate helpful action.

YOU ARE UNIQUE AND SPECIAL

How much do you really respect and value yourself? Are you aware of how much you tend to underrate yourself? In this busy, computerized age it's easy to feel unimportant, unrecognized as an individual person, especially if you are part of a large organization or family. You have many features, qualities and abilities that are unique to you. The truth is that you are very precious as an individual human being. You don't need to compare yourself to others: being true to yourself is the best way you can live your life. You are important. What you need and want is important. Always remember that you are special.

Developing self-esteem is based on valuing yourself. It means being gentle with yourself and respecting yourself. We are not talking here about confidence tricks to try to fool other people when you're feeling awful inside, nor tips for making the 'right' impression when you're not being true to yourself. Genuine self-esteem is valuing and respecting yourself at a deep level and most people need to learn how to do this. Another aspect of self-esteem is learning to use and trust your personal intuition, those hunches which will guide you to what is appropriate for you. With high self-esteem what you want to do with your life is important, how you spend your time and energy on a daily basis is important. You take time to discover what it is you want to achieve. You take action that is appropriate for you and want to treat yourself well.

You have many talents, many ways of thinking and doing things. The exact combination is what makes you special. This makes comparing yourself with others pointless. You cannot say that they are better than you are or vice versa. Nobody will ever be a better you than you! We see so many examples of really competent, able people who yet lack self-belief and self-value. Even when you know you are capable of doing something you need the self-esteem to follow through and persevere with what is important to you. There are a relatively small number of brilliant people and of really stupid people; there is a whole expanse of people of a similar level of capability yet with varied achievements and degrees of success. Most people could learn to be successful at one or more of many things, depending on interest level and the level of self-belief and self-value. Over and over again on our programmes we see confidence and self-esteem as the decisive factor in success – both in getting started in the first place and in persevering with what needs to be done.

Once you believe in yourself enough to really want to be successful you need to add self-value. It is important to value yourself enough to take the steps, with thinking that is helpful to you, as well as practical action, to ensure you achieve the success you want. You are already a valuable and worthwhile person. Value yourself enough to make any adjustments to your thinking and behaviour that would be beneficial to your development and success.

You have within you a deep desire to fulfil your potential, which is unique to you. This is an important part of self-esteem. You can never experience full self-esteem or happiness unless you listen to your personal intuition to acknowledge what you want to and can do. You have within you the potential to achieve something very special in your life. You have the ability to express fully the individual human being you are. What an opportunity to be yourself, to let yourself be the best you can be. Just think, there can never be another you. You are absolutely unique and special.

I always remember I am special.

PERSONAL FOCUS

Believe In and Value Yourself

1 Write down three ways in which you feel your life would be different if you totally believed in yourself.

2 Write down three new goals you would set for yourself and the practical steps you need to take to put them into place. Remember you can continue to expand any of your ideas in your notebook.

3 What are three new ways you would choose to act?

4 Describe a situation which is proving challenging, where you need to remind yourself of your true value. Your true value includes your qualities and abilities, particularly those things that are special to you. Write these out and remind yourself of them.

5 With added self-value, what will you do, improve on, in your life? Describe the steps you'd take.

RELAXATION

Strengthening Self-Belief and Self-Value

Sit or lie in a comfortable position where you will not be disturbed. Take a couple of comfortable breaths and let the relaxation move throughout your body. As you relax, let go of self-doubt. Bring in a feeling of belief in yourself. What would it feel like? Notice how good it would feel to believe in yourself, to trust yourself to be able to handle any situation. An important part of valuing yourself is listening to yourself, to that part of you, your personal intuition, which knows what is best for you as a unique individual human being. This link can feel strong when you relax and feel in touch with yourself. Have you any hunches about what it is important for you to have and do in your life? Remember what it feels like to feel so relaxed and confident. Then, if you begin to feel tense, you can remind yourself of that saying, 'I believe in myself!', 'I am of great value!' during the day.

SECTION FOUR

Self-Esteem and Your Relationships

CHAPTER SEVEN

Relating to Others

You will have known long before you picked up this book that feeling happy or upset in your relationships with others is guaranteed to affect your self-esteem, perhaps more than anything else. When things are going well in your relationships – personal, social and at work – you tend to feel good and your self-esteem is high. However, when you are having problems or challenges in one or more of these areas you can feel wretched and your self-esteem will be low. Practically every aspect of your life involves you in relating to other people so there is a link here with your self-esteem on a daily basis. In short, our relationships – particularly those closest to us – are one of the means both to great joy and to great pain. It's natural to have close, intimate relationships with others. We always feel better when we do, and life's not much fun when we don't!

So whether you're married, separated, divorced, single, a person with young children or grandchildren, or a young person setting out in life, the use of self-esteem in developing loving and joyful relationships is essential.

All your life involves relationships, with yourself first, then with other people – with members of your family, parents, your personal partner, children, with your friends, colleagues, customers, neighbours, people who run the local shops, those you meet at social activities or sports.

You have many special things to give in your relationships with other people. However, it is important to have a good relationship with yourself first by keeping your self-esteem high and trusting your personal intuition. Then you can get to know what is appropriate for you. It is important to know what is right for you at any time and what suits you best.

My high self-esteem leads me to fulfilling relationships.

HANDLING CHANGING RELATIONSHIPS

Are you faced with a changing relationship? Many relationships are changing at this time: marriages and close relationships that people thought would last are falling apart or changing. There seem to be more people moving out of relationships, including marriage, sometimes into another one and sometimes to be on their own. You may be feeling low and dispirited as a result of a marriage break-up or relationship difficulties. If you are in this situation, know that although it feels awful now you will feel better. There is a lot that you can do to help yourself.

You may feel yourself going into a slump, feeling either numb with upset or very angry and tearful. This is the stage to take things a day at a time, get yourself feeling as relaxed as you can each day. Come back to your belief in yourself. Remind yourself that things are working out for the best although it feels awful now. Each day you are getting stronger. This is the time for supportive friends and to do some self-esteem work with yourself or with a friend. You need something and someone that won't just add to your upset. You don't want constant agreement from other people, for example, that a situation or person is awful.

It is tempting to get caught up in blaming. However, that achieves nothing and just causes more ill-feeling as well as pain to yourself. Moving through the misery of blaming is a process you can both initiate and accelerate. Because you will find that *the process of letting go of blaming* is one of the most important and helpful things a person can learn, it is outlined below:

- First tell the truth to yourself – that you feel hurt over your relationship with the person concerned.

- Then, and it's best to be on your own for this, write out all the things you feel that person has done and said to hurt you. Get these all out of your system. Tell yourself just how you have felt or feel about what has happened, whether that is angry, sad or frightened. Keep breathing in a relaxed way.

- Now you need to call on your courage to make a leap of the heart to help you, and the question is 'Are you willing to stop blaming the other person? To give up your resentment towards them?' Your blaming of them is what is keeping you tied, bonded to them; if you want peace of mind you won't get it until you do give up the blaming. What you need is at least the willingness to stop blaming. Tell yourself you are now ready to do this, to let go of your resentment and so bring back your energy and attention to focus on your life and yourself to the fullest. While you are holding out for revenge you'll never have peace of mind! You may want to put forward a statement of your intention: 'I now release myself from blaming this person, I'm now at peace with regard to my relationship with . . .'

- You will need to do this last part of the process each day for a number of days, letting go of the other's offences as they come to your awareness, feeling lighter and more joyful every day as you do so. Whether you see the person regularly in your life or never, the process will work and needs to be done to release *you*.

- If you're in a continuing relationship you may want to communicate your feelings and your needs, wants and expectations. You will do so more clearly and effectively if you've started to clear the offences out of your heart first. Be gentle with yourself, doing things you enjoy. In as far as you can, be gentle with the other person involved, too. Stopping blaming will help you by setting your own energy and emotions and attention free. Work on your self-esteem and put your attention on what is important to you.

I begin to let go and move through this experience.

You Can Survive Separation

When you have separated from a person it takes some time for your full recovery. Meanwhile, as best you can, while always acknowledging your feelings, let yourself be comforted, then focus and re-focus on yourself and what is important to you, what you want to achieve. Put some attention on areas you may have neglected – friends, family, looking after your body – and vary your surroundings. Get away, if not for a full holiday, for a weekend or a day.

It is best that you stay separated and avoid contact while you are feeling vulnerable, because you may not get the answers and the comfort that you want. You need to be ready for a 'Yes' or a 'No' from this person. If this is not possible, due to practical arrangements with regard to children, then try to minimize the contact.

When you are going through a difficult time emotionally, supportive friends are essential. Have them with you for practicalities, eg helping to move, to make things easier for you. This is not to say you won't move through painful emotions too, because you will. That is far more beneficial than experiencing the long-term effects of trying to hold them at bay or suppressing your feelings altogether.

When you separate from someone you've been living with, who has been a part of your daily life for some time, however acrimonious the parting, you are bound to feel a void. You cannot work out what will happen or even at this stage what you want to happen. There's bound to be a settling down process where your mixed thoughts and feelings level out. So focus on yourself and your work, look after yourself, be with friends and family, let yourself be comforted. Do not deny the emotional pain yet do not make it a continual focus. Above all make a space for a quiet time each day with yourself. Listen to your personal intuition for guidance and support. Remember to ask and be open to that assistance and it will come. Just listen. Write it down and act on it.

When you feel low or have regrets and are reminded of things you wanted to do together, for example, travel, holidays, work, or of the beautiful place you must leave because it is no longer your home, have courage. Listen to your intuition with regard to what's best for you now. Don't kid yourself that occasional good times make up for the daily grind of a relationship that isn't working. You can now begin to set yourself free.

I am now free to move forward with my life.

MOVING THROUGH LONELINESS

Many people are feeling lonely right now. Sometimes we feel isolated, sad, out of touch, whether or not there are people for us to be with in our life. When you feel you haven't got people or a person you can be open and honest with, you often feel lonely, even if there are various people around you. Sometimes we do all sorts of things to avoid admitting to ourselves, 'Yes I feel lonely.' Instead, we often sleep long hours, go out to things we've got no real interest in, watch television night after night, spend time with people not because we love to be with them but because we hate to be alone. Having people around and being with people doesn't always make you feel less lonely. Very often you feel worse when you're not with them if you've been using children, a spouse or a lover to fill a gap. When we acknowledge to ourselves that we feel lonely or are afraid of feeling lonely, that begins to shift the unpleasant feeling right away.

Once you realize that you are feeling lonely, the first step is to ask yourself if there is something you can give yourself that will bring you joy or ease, for example, more time to relax or a way you can make your body more comfortable. Listen to your personal intuition. Check if there is anything important with regard to your life that you need to do. Have you been receiving whisperings, hints and ideas from yourself that you've perhaps been ignoring? Never forget that you are special, your life is precious. What you want is important. Find out what that is with regard to yourself. Put your attention on *you*. This won't make you selfish, and it will stop you always trying to get attention from others to fill that gap for you.

At the same time as you are looking after your own energy, you can see where you can extend yourself with regard to others. For example, if you want more warmth, support and companionship, see where you can give that to yourself and then you can look for a way of extending that to others. See where you can reach out and make new friends as well as re-energizing established friendships. Remember, the more you enjoy your own company, the more others will enjoy it!

WHEN YOU WOULD RATHER BE IN LOVE

So you are smitten! Yet the object of your affection doesn't seem to be – at least by you. Desperation sets in and self-esteem slumps, so what to do? When you're putting your love and attention out to a person and it's not returned, don't take it personally: they may be fearful, confused and perhaps also married to someone else! Relax and congratulate yourself for having such passionate feelings – they're coming from you. By being open, you open yourself up to this relationship or another even better one. Enjoy feeling the feelings and communicate them if appropriate, for *you're* experiencing these feelings whether your 'beloved' is or not. When you feel these fully, remind yourself that you are the most important person in your life; draw all of your energy back to yourself. *Make* yourself focus on yourself, your life and what is important and enjoyable to you. Ensure that you're seeing and enjoying being with other people. Difficult as it may seem, just be willing to let go of this person. Think about yourself instead. Get really involved again in yourself and your life. If you let this person go, he or she may return to you if it's right, or someone better will appear in time.

If it's appropriate, you can communicate what you are feeling. You can say what you'd like. However, you need to feel content in yourself anyway, regardless of the response you get. Remember it's not good for you to keep putting out your love and attention where it doesn't seem to be appreciated and wanted. Rather put it where it's welcomed and wanted.

It's lovely to have a partner, a lover in your life, a special person. Yet there will be times when you don't, times when it is more appropriate that, for example, you are totally focused on your work. You can turn to other sources of giving and receiving support and affection, such as friends, family and colleagues. It is always good, even in a close relationship, to have that balance of exchange with other people as well; this lifts the burden from that other person to be everything to you and for you to be everything to them. However close you become to another person, you still have your 'purpose' for your life to follow. Each person is responsible for himself or herself.

However, if you're not 'in love' right now, you're probably wishing you were – unless you're through with romance for this week! Everyone loves that heightened sense of appreciation of ourselves, of life and of being loved that comes with a romantic relationship. We love the intimacy and the fun. However, you don't need to wait for a new 'romantic relationship' or a transformation of your current one to experience that sparkle. Notice the romance in your everyday life with the people you are with regularly or occasionally.

Notice the specialness of your interchanges with those at work and in your neighbourhood. All of life becomes romantic as you experience your own uniqueness and the specialness of other people.

I now let my life be romantic.

Have Helpful Thoughts about Your Relationships

It will help you so much in the area of relationships, as in other areas, to focus on what is working and what you *do* like. If you keep thinking about and focusing on what's wrong with a person, they'll seem more and more like that. So often appreciation felt and expressed will make a world of difference. It's easy to get out of the habit of expressing appreciation to the person we are closest to. You know yourself how much you love to be appreciated, to be told how well you're doing or how much you're liked. Other people do too. As you hold to the good about a person, you give them the chance to become more like that, benefiting them and you!

It makes sense when you want to improve the relationships in your life and to draw in new, better relationships, to notice what your own thoughts about yourself are in relationships. Are you going around with thoughts like 'I always get hurt/left/rejected', 'Relationships mess up my work', 'Relationships are exhausting', 'Women are not to be trusted', 'Women are devious and use men', 'Men are unreliable', 'I am unattractive to men or women', 'Men or women restrict my freedom or power', 'People don't treat me with respect'? If you are experiencing any of these thoughts as deeply held truths for you, then that is what will tend to be your experience. For example, a woman who thinks that 'men are unreliable' will take it personally if a man changes or alters an arrangement because he is actually ill with flu!

It is more beneficial to think helpful thoughts such as 'My relationships with men/women are joyful and energizing', 'I trust people and they support me', 'Men are reliable and supportive', 'My relationships last', 'I'm attractive to men/women', 'I have freedom and intimacy in my relationships', 'People treat me with respect', 'I'm loved for doing what is best for me'. Now with thoughts like this your experience will inevitably be better. As with all deeply held beliefs, we need to continually remind ourselves this is the way we want it to be from now on. It makes so much sense, if you want improvements in a new relationship and in those you already have, to improve your thoughts.

LOOK FORWARD TO MEETING NEW PEOPLE

You must first make the decision that you want to meet new people. You need to be open to meeting new people, to making new friends, perhaps to meeting that special person. Do you feel you are lacking in confidence, worried about what people think of you? Then do your self-esteem work. Allow yourself to be the person you want to be – for example, a healthy, attractive, successful person sought after and loved by many. How would such a person behave? You don't need to totally revamp your image although you may choose to try a new look. However, if you know the sorts of things you look good in, then wear them. Start your new wardrobe from where it is. Make sure you have plenty of things ready to go out in to these new social occasions!

As you remind yourself that you're a wonderful person, you can then quietly and confidently go out and meet other people, not feeling you need to impress them. You can relax and put your attention on them; certainly you can take the initiative where appropriate, by contributing to the conversation. If you are relaxed, people will find you easy to be with. They will like you even more if you listen attentively to *them*!

I now relax and enjoy being myself.

See where you can take the initiative with regard to other people. It's easier where you have a shared interest. You may need to be the one who makes the phonecalls, makes the suggestions and puts out invitations to get the ball rolling as other people may not get round to it for all sorts of reasons. They may be under stress, nervous that you may reject them, or they may simply be very busy. You may be the one to make the overtures, to whoever you want to spend time with, whether that's one person or several other people. Initially, start with situations you can easily handle, such as an invitation for a cup of coffee or lunch out rather than a five-course dinner cooked by you! As you relax, your natural sense of fun, not forced jollity, will come through. Be yourself. A calm, positive, cheerful outlook will attract friends. Don't wait for people to invite you to be part of the 'action', create it for yourself!

MAINTAINING CLOSE RELATIONSHIPS

All relationships, particularly romantic ones, require maintenance. They require acceptance of the other person and a delight in being with that person. You need a sense of security, to be able to share important aims with each other, and to have a willingness to communicate openly and helpfully. This last, communicating openly and helpfully, is vital to maintaining intimacy.

I remember to listen.

Relationships in which love lasts are those in which there is intimacy, letting the other person see what you are really feeling. Don't let time go by without communicating with your partner. Updating on what you're both feeling is important in keeping your relationships alive and intimate. This needs to be combined with putting your attention on all the good, supportive aspects of your partner. Resentment kills off love. Deal with it by letting go of the continual blaming, judging or criticizing that you might be doing, either out loud or in your mind.

This is not to say that you shouldn't sometimes show your vulnerable side and admit that you are afraid or confused. When you don't tell people the truth, they can't relate to the true you. It's a question of balance. People don't want to hear time after time that you are, for example, tired, nervous, angry.

In an intimate relationship you will want your partner to care for your feelings, to behave in a way that is appropriate and supportive and good for you. Things can be talked through and changed for the better so that both people feel supported and fulfilled.

PERSONAL FOCUS

Before you do this set of exercises, you may want to complete or repeat the process on letting go of blaming given on p 73.

Handling Relationship Difficulties

1 At some stage, when you've acknowledged all of your feelings, you may need to just keep letting them go, by writing them down and scoring them out. (You may want to complete again the exercise on Free Yourself from Blaming on p 37.)

2 When you experience an unexpected change in a relationship, particularly if undesired, treat yourself for shock physically, mentally and emotionally, because you may feel confused or dazed. Write down all you can do for yourself at this time.

3 Plan some quiet times with yourself. When can these be? What is one thing you can do that will help restore your balance?

4 Which of your friends and family would be most supportive for you right now (other than the person you are having a problem with)?

5 Resolutely, determinedly, put your attention on other things, those things that are important to you, that give you joy and assist you in your purpose. List these and tick them off as you put them in place.

Helpful Thoughts For Relationships

1 Write out some of your unhelpful thoughts about relationships.

Now change these unhelpful thoughts to helpful ones, eg 'I meet men who are intelligent, attractive and supportive!' 'Women listen to me and let me choose what I want to do', 'Relationships are fun!' Keep repeating these thoughts and bring in the feeling of what it would be like to have them true.

2 When you catch yourself thinking or saying something unsupportive, change that right away! List your new thoughts below.

What I Want in a Relationship

Write out what you really want in a relationship without specifying a particular person. This will include some of the qualities the person will have; what you want in your relationship with that person eg a home together, children; what you want for yourself, independently of that relationship eg to see your own friends, to continue to build your career.

RELAXATIONS

Letting Go Of Fear

Go through your usual relaxation procedure. Feel the fear and hurt feelings dissolving without trying to analyse them. Without trying to work out in detail what you're going to do, just ask for help, support and guidance; feel that connection with your personal intuition which will help you to move forward with courage.

A Wonderful Relationship

Following the steps for relaxation, envisage your life as becoming more fulfilling. Listen to your personal intuition with regard to what you *really* want in a relationship. Relax and allow yourself to imagine what would be wonderful for you. Record below.

Communication, Criticism and Conflict

SUPPORTIVE COMMUNICATIONS

Kind, open communication is important for keeping relationships warm and loving. Letting people know how you feel about the things that concern and please you, all assist in keeping a relationship close. When you want to discuss a problem with another person it is best to do this on the day it happens rather than letting it drag on so that further misunderstandings arise.

People have different approaches to life. Don't assume they see things from your point of view or that they understand how you feel or what you want. Tell them, yet don't expect them to change right away (or ever) to your way of seeing things. Be prepared to listen to how they think and feel about things. Work out how you can help each other towards a solution, without one person doing something they don't want to do.

While you don't need to know exactly why you're feeling a particular way, it's important that you remember that you're not always upset for the reason you think. Very often old hurts are triggered off by what another person says or does.

It is really easy when you feel hurt or exasperated, especially with those you are very close to, to shout, explode with rage and say all sorts of things that you later regret, yet which sometimes remain in the heart of the other person. While it's best of all to integrate your emotions and keep communicating on a daily basis, sometimes things build up and a small argument can become a full-scale row. Matching angry energy, as we know, doesn't work!

So as not to cause an argument, or because feelings are so sensitive, you may try to push down the feelings or emotions that you think will be painful. When we do this our feelings don't flow, move through us and change, but rather stay stuck there. Acknowledge your feelings at least to yourself and they will change and move. Often too, out of loyalty – a feeling of us against the world – we do not say how we really feel. Our partner is our ally and we fear losing his or her affection. What we need to do is to respect our own and our partner's innermost feelings.

Always focus on what is working in your relationship – what is right, what is good, the positive points. Continue daily to let go of blaming. Especially in an intimate relation-ship, be gentle with yourself and the other person.

PROJECTING GOODWILL HELPS COMMUNICATION

Goodwill is an essential element in all our communications with people, perhaps especially when we may fear the other person is not going to like what we have to say. One of the most important things that people want to be shown is respect. When we show them this respect, especially when not agreeing with them or telling them something they initially may not want to hear, a more beneficial result is likely.

If you are angry, it's better to integrate this rather than suppress it or come out with a totally uncontrolled expression of your anger. You will feel worse about this than if you had not said anything. Sometimes you may need to go through the process already described of getting the offences out of your system and letting go of blaming (p. 73). On other occasions a short walk around the block will suffice. Remember, your self-esteem goal is always peace of mind rather than exacting revenge. So when you think about a forthcoming meeting you can set the tone by bringing goodwill into the picture.

I now respect myself and others in all my communications.

If you let yourself be pushed around you will end up resenting people. You may have to counter brush-offs and sometimes you may not get what you ask for. You will, however, feel better for having expressed your feelings and wishes. Remember to have some degree of flexibility built in if you are asking someone to do something you want. Your underlying level of goodwill is important. If you are communicating what you want, keep stating what you want and do not get side-tracked. If you're presenting how you feel, be sure to own your emotions and be specific; for example, 'When you do such-and-such I feel . . .', rather than 'You make me so angry when you do such-and-such'. You may also have to counter suggestions that you are making a fuss or over-reacting by saying 'I don't feel that I am – this is important to me.'

I say clearly what is important to me.

If you want someone to improve or change it helps to make suggestions or ask questions rather than just telling them what you want them to do. It's also important to really listen without passing judgement while a person is speaking. If appropriate you can indicate that you appreciate they are feeling upset. Sometimes with aggressive individuals who everybody wants to shut up, it can help to ask them, 'Is there anything else you want to say?' That can work because they are so unused to people wanting to listen to them.

I listen to people.

Sometimes we don't communicate directly and clearly because we get so hooked into our need for approval, worrying more about what others think and feel than our own thoughts and feelings. We become unable to act or speak up for ourselves, even when it's appropriate or essential for our wellbeing that we do so. Remember, in most cases you don't need to explain your life to other people, especially when it doesn't affect them in any way. Choose what is appropriate for you. Your choice of hairstyle, clothes, holiday, companions needs no explanation, nor does it really matter what others think. Nor do you need to allow other people to try to evoke a sense of guilt in order to manipulate you: 'I want you to do this and if you don't it means you don't love me, you aren't a good friend.' Be your own judge, but not in a critical sense.

When we constantly put other peoples' opinions and feelings before our own, we diminish our self-esteem and our power. We know at a deep level that we're not honouring ourselves, that there is something uncentred in the way we are behaving. We also put out the message that other people's feelings and opinions are more important than our own. We then get treated in this way and complain that our thoughts and feelings have not been taken into consideration by others.

You can be very truthful with yourself yet you'll be more effective if you're tactfully truthful with other people. Likewise, it's not your role to sit in judgement on other people and their behaviour, however strange it may seem to you!

I approve of my choices.

YOU CAN HANDLE CRITICISM

Often the manner in which criticism comes across is as hurtful as what is said. Sometimes, although the information is correct, for example, it would have been more appropriate to have done something a different way, it is the coldness, anger or apparent resentment that are communicated that can be so hurtful.

Think how you could have handled things differently and don't be defensive. Say how you feel and make appropriate comments with appropriate action. Criticism tends to feed self-doubt and, while not wanting to be blind to changes that it would serve us to make, you need to come back to a strong belief in yourself.

When you face angry criticism, especially if it's of a threatening nature, know first that the person is angry *per se* – if you had not triggered that anger someone else would have done! Comply with their demands only if it's appropriate to you, and don't feel you need to change your behaviour to suit them unless, on review, you feel you want to. If you feel very upset, do some self-esteem work and get yourself feeling as good as possible, then you can more clearly decide what you want to do and say. Be appropriate, especially if the angry person is your boss at work! You may also congratulate yourself that things that used to upset you no longer do. There is no need to speak angrily to the other person, just relax and let it go. Have such criticisms make you softer and gentler, not harder and more fearful.

I approve of myself especially if others are critical.

When You Feel Trapped in a Situation

What do you do if you feel bludgeoned by a bad-tempered spouse who's providing a roof over your head and money to live on? This is tricky to say the least and, while you cannot tolerate actual physical violence, you may need to work around the other person and situation. Do all you can to keep your self-esteem and energy high. Everything seems better when you feel better about yourself. While doing what you can to find a way of living peacefully, be open to having an escape route, whether that is by saving your own money or by having someone to stay with.

While it is preferable to be financially independent, for

women in particular, this is not always the case, and for many with a child or children it means relying on benefits, perhaps some money from part-time work and support, whether financial or otherwise, from friends and family.

Look for small ways where you can be independent, where you can feel free, where you can be grateful for your situation. Focus determinedly on these, however small, and look for ways you can expand them. Start doing some joyful thing for yourself each day. With regard to money, start saving a small amount each week, even if your budget is really small, to spend on something that's not a necessity, that is a pleasure to you.

Keep letting go of resentment – a big challenge! – and focusing on what you want. Keep changing your thoughts, let your emotions flow and integrate. Fit in that relaxation time. Also pay attention to diet, moderate exercise, rest and fresh air. All these will strengthen you. Remember your own self-esteem and a warm supportive network are most important of all to you.

HANDLING DIFFICULT PEOPLE

There's no doubt about it, from time to time you'll come across people who are angry, bad-tempered, unpleasant and disagreeable. If you can be big enough not to be drawn into arguments with such people you'll save yourself a lot of time and energy. So if you sometimes receive an unhelpful or unkind remark from someone, in a shop or from one of your business suppliers or whoever, just let it go. Even agreeing with them can totally take the sting out of the situation! It is only if you're always getting aggression and unhelpful, angry responses from others that you could usefully look at whether there might be within you something that prompts such unhelpful reactions. However, for the casual unhelpful encounter, just relax and let go of the unpleasantness when you leave the shop or office.

Remember again, the more obnoxious a person is, the

more screwed up he or she is inside. If people don't respect themselves they won't respect others either! There may well be times when you find yourself dealing with such people – people who are even malicious and abusive, intent on deliberately causing harm to others. However difficult it can seem in an unfair or threatening situation, it is important to pull back your emotions and energy from it, to be able to get on with important aspects of your life. Remember, the angrier people become the more helpless they are feeling. Assume they are behaving as they are from low self-esteem, inner disturbance and upset. The challenge for you is to remain poised and unaffected yet able to defend or protect your rights. To be able to do that effectively, you need to focus on the facts, not the emotion around them.

So the first step is to release your own feelings of anger, frustration and blaming. The next step is to clarify the facts. What are your real rights in the situation? See it as a situation to move through rather than an emotional issue. It can seem difficult to do this when there are distractions. However, remember you don't need to get caught in endless arguments on aspects of the situation which aren't even important to you – draw back your energy.

I let go of grievances and make room for more good things in my life.

Bullies are often frightened people with low self-esteem who have got their way by frightening or intimidating other people. They are constantly on the defensive as well as the offensive to exercise what they see as their power, though really they are expressing a fearful mode of existence. While these individuals may have become disturbed for a number of reasons, they are unpleasant to deal with and when you can avoid them do so. Yet do not be intimidated.

If you're being harassed, perhaps by neighbours or at work, come from a point of calm self-esteem however distressed you may feel. Get the support of friends, family or colleagues. Keep to the facts of the situation, outline what has occurred and what you now require to be done. Where possible bring what is happening to the public arena. Sometimes you'll be able to join with others; sometimes you'll be on your own and need to get advice to defend your rights.

However, ask friends for support on a personal level and perhaps those in authority or with experience for other aspects.

It is essential that you keep your own thoughts high and stay focused on what is important to you. However, notice there are people who do not necessarily share your high intentions and ideals. They may be downright malicious or simply thoughtless, not caring about the effects their behaviour has on others and determined to continue to do what suits them.

When you do feel judgmental of others, let go, and draw your attention firmly back to yourself. Focus on what you want to achieve and what you can do for yourself to help you feel good. Learn to let go of any situation that doesn't seem harmonious. If it is a social situation shut the door on it when you leave the event. It can sometimes take determination to pull your thoughts away, yet it is excellent to do this and the only way to move forward.

It's vital to look after yourself, to get on with what is important in your life, and pull your energy back to you. Regard the upset with the other person as an irritation – no more, no less. You are the most important person in your life. On the physical level include relaxation and then ensure that your thoughts are supportive. Write out your goals with regard to what is important to you. Look at what practical steps you can now take.

I now refocus with double strength on myself and what is important to me.

PERSONAL FOCUS

Supportive Communication

Clarify what you want to communicate to another person and write out your message. Check that you have been as kind as you can, both to the other person and yourself. Also identify what you feel and why, and what you'd like the other person to do: for example, 'When you . . . I feel . . ., What I'd like you to do is . . .'.

Handling Criticism

1 Notice and record three ways in which you can in your thoughts and actions be less critical and more appreciative of both yourself and others.

2 When you have been criticized, acknowledge to yourself how you are feeling. Now separate out the practical aspects of any criticism from your emotions. Look at what you might do differently if appropriate. Outline your comments.

Handling a Difficult Person or Situation

1 Outline how you feel about the person or situation.

2 Having accepted your feelings, let them go for the moment (if they are still strong, review the freeing yourself from blaming exercises, p. 37). Describe the situation as just that: a situation.

3 What outcome do you want?

4 What can you do for your part? What practical steps can you take? Who can help you?

5 Once you have done what you can, bring all of your attention back to yourself. Reflect on what is important to you. Outline below.

RELAXATIONS

Projecting Goodwill

Relax. See yourself in your mind's eye relaxed and feeling good. Send out goodwill in advance to any person or group of people you are going to be communicating with. Particularly when there's any disharmony, send out goodwill in advance for harmony and a good outcome to the communication.

Feel Free and Move Forward

Relax. See yourself in your mind's eye moving ahead. See yourself free of the influence of other people, moving ahead now. Use any anger you feel to propel you forward. See and experience, feel yourself to be successful and joyful. Just take a moment to let in or experience all that you would expect to feel successful and joyful. What would that mean to you? What would that feel like to you?

CHAPTER NINE

The Family and Young People

Every member of a family needs to be given love and respect for themselves as individuals. It doesn't work for the child to be given priority at the expense of the adults, so they cannot maintain their self-esteem and do what is important to them. That only leads to resentment and doesn't provide a demonstration of how to value yourself and do what is right and best for you. Nor, of course, is it right for the child to be squashed or bullied in any way, for children need to be encouraged to respect themselves and others. Treating a child without respect leads to all kinds of damage, not only to the individual young person but ultimately to society. It is not important what form the family takes. It is the respect shown and experienced that is the important factor.

Learning to respect others begins when a child is young. The process of mutual respect, caring and encouragement provides the model for the future with regard to interacting, living and working harmoniously with others. Teenagers in particular need respect, especially when they are rebellious and unappealing, but they must also have a clear understanding that they must respect others too.

The best thing you can do for your children, in addition to loving and providing for them, is to build and live your life from a point of high self-esteem. Children and young people need a demonstration from adults, preferably their parents, of high self-esteem, of how to respect themselves and other people.

My high self-esteem is best for all of my family.

HIGH SELF-ESTEEM IS IMPORTANT FOR YOUNG PEOPLE

If you're a young person reading this, you may be feeling particularly confused with regard to what is of value, what is important in your life. You have inherited a system, or a lack of one, a way of relating to others, and the world passed on to you by previous generations which may not seem helpful. So it may be difficult for you to get your bearings as to what is important to you.

In this confusion, you may doubt yourself and feel you are not important. You may not value or respect yourself fully. You may not want to take responsibility or may want to take responsibility but be at a loss to know how. The first necessary step is to stop blaming others – parents, teachers, friends or the government. While it may seem as though they have been unhelpful they have probably been doing their best. Begin to look at what you can do for yourself. An important part of this is looking at how you think, speak and act. Is how you think and act helpful to yourself and others? Are you being the sort of person you want to be?

It is important that you know you are of great value, irreplaceable, wonderful, unique. Always put your attention on what is good about yourself and others. You may need to ask yourself what is important to you in your life. How can you respect yourself and others more? Looking at society as it is, you may not get many answers or those you get may be unhelpful. So when you do something, look at what feels right to *you*. When you think about what you want to achieve, you begin to understand about how you feel in yourself, about what is right for you and what is not. What would be the best way for you to spend your life? Start to consider this. This is your life.

I now value myself and my life.

SELF-ESTEEM CAN HELP WITH ADDICTIONS

Many young people have feelings of low self-worth, a lack of a sense of purpose and the desire to escape their current feelings and replace them with a buzz. This leads them to take drugs. One of the drugs taken, crack cocaine, is particularly effective at suppressing feelings, and with them the individual's true sense of self-worth and personal intuition.

If you or someone you know is committed to getting out of an addictive drug habit, first make sure you have support for those times when you feel drawn to getting back into drug use. Concentrate on improving your health. It's important to somehow get through a day at a time rather than looking too far ahead. Start to listen to yourself and what's best for you. Working on your self-esteem, discovering what you want to do with your life, the work you want to do, is essential. Get some work, if possible, and money that enables you to live with some respect for yourself. It will help you to build up a network of people you want to be like, eg non-drug-users. Then you can rebuild your links within the family that may have been torn apart by your drug habit.

When I want respect I start by respecting myself.

TAKE RESPONSIBILITY FOR YOUR OWN HAPPINESS

Who is responsible for your happiness. Who is responsible for your husband's, your wife's, your child's, your colleague's happiness? You may have already learned that you alone are responsible for whether you are happy in your life or not, or you may still believe that someone else can or should 'make you happy'. While it's always better if we are as supportive, compassionate and helpful as we can be to each other, each of us as we grow into adulthood is responsible for himself or herself. Without the tools for building self-esteem it can seem very difficult to know what to do. However, you now know how to use your thoughts, emotions and imagination as well as your personal intuition. Building your self-esteem is something you must do for yourself. No one else can do it for you.

When we feel we are to blame for another person's unhappiness then we entrap ourselves into feeling guilty. That helps neither them nor us and in time we may feel resentful about this 'bind'. So treat people with respect and encourage them to speak well and think well of themselves and others, and then draw your attention back to yourself.

Feelings of dissatisfaction come from within. It's never too late to focus your attention on your needs. What could you do for yourself that will assist you in feeling better? How can you improve your relationships to have them warmer and more loving? The most important part of you is your personal intuition and you need to listen to it so you can take appropriate action in order that you feel happy and fulfilled. Keeping yourself feeling centred, joyful and purposeful provides a demonstration of high self-esteem.

I now listen to my personal intuition on what is best for me.

It is easy to waste energy by being caught up in distractions, things that are not really important. Even dearly loved friends and family can deplete our energy if we're constantly worrying about them instead of putting our attention. 'What is the most important use of my time?' is a question for you to ask yourself each day. No one else can do this for you. Keep an hour-by-hour check on what you are doing with your precious energy and time. Once you have a sense of what you want to achieve, it's easier to know how you should use your time and energy. You will only feel fulfilled when you are doing what is important to you and gives you joy. Sometimes what is best for you is working and completing some project; other times it's having a drink and watching TV. For high self-esteem, fulfilment and peace of mind it is your personal intuition that you need to pay attention to.

Be true to yourself. Know that giving and receiving goes on on many levels! One person in the relationship may provide more financially and materially, another may provide more in practical terms or in terms of mental and emotional support. Many women nowadays complain of losing their identity in a relationship, particularly when they're financially dependent. Equally, many men feel pressurized to be the financial supplier in a relationship, leading to low self-esteem. Feeling obligated to do certain things, when these are not in your best interests, does not honour you or the other person. So if you're financially supported, do not judge yourself. Keep centred and balanced at all times so you have nothing to regret or feel resentful about.

In your relationships it is so important to keep yourself feeling good, to do what is best for *you*. You may need to make adjustments to suit your partner and children, in a way that does not undermine your own self-esteem. They then do not have the 'burden' of trying to cheer you up, and you also allow them the freedom to do what they want to keep themselves happy. When you are happy, you provide a demonstration for your partner, family and friends that they too can do this for themselves.

Everyone benefits when I am happy.

Personal Focus

High Self-Esteem in the Family

1 What is one way you can show love and respect for yourself?

2 What is one way you can show love and respect for someone in your family?

3 What is one way you can ask for love and respect to be shown to you by your family?

For Young People

1 What do you want to do with your life? How would you like your life to be? Listen to your hunches, dreams or daydreams. Write them down.

2 Talk to people who are doing the sort of work you feel attracted to. Make enquiries about, for example, training you will need to get. Keep a notebook or put on tape or computer your ideas of things that interest you, that you may feel you'd like to work at.

3 What is the first step you can take now with regard to how you would like your world to be? Is there an organization you can join. If your concerns are for the environment what can you do, at home or school, for example, to save energy or recycle things?

4 Notice what works for *you* to keep your self-esteem high. Listen to your personal intuition and your hunches. Record them in your notebook or on your computer.

Creating Satisfaction and Enjoyment

Relax and do this.

1 List all the things you can do that give you satisfaction and a sense of moving forward with your life. Set a time and date when you're going to do them.

2 What can you do with your partner or friend or a family member that would be joyful and fun for both of you? Again, set a time and date when you will do this.

Relaxations

High Self-Esteem in the Family

Relax and see yourself in your mind's eye loving and respecting yourself. See every member of your family feeling self-respect and self-esteem. Feel your love and respect for them moving out towards them. Now feel the love and respect your family have for you moving back to you. Be open to receiving it.

For Young People

Relaxing in your body is essential for learning to relax in your mind and helpful in letting you feel your feelings without discomfort. It also gives you energy. So get quiet in a room on your own. Soothing music may assist you. Arrange not to be interrupted and relax your body just bit by bit. See a picture in your mind of a place where you can be relaxed and quiet, a beautiful place in nature. Notice how calm and centred you are, how being there builds your self-esteem. When you're relaxed and centred, is there anything you would like to know? You can ask your personal intuition a question. It may be about the next step for you to take in some area of your life. Gently open your eyes before you get up, feeling soothed, yet alert.

Creating More Joy in Your Life

Relax, see yourself full of self-esteem and happy. Notice what that feels like. Notice what you're doing that contributes to your joy. Who are you with? What sort of surroundings are you in? Send out lines of goodwill to draw these happy circumstances to you. Listen to your personal intuition to see what it is most important for you to know and to do with regard to your happiness. Look forward to doing more of what is joyful for you, as you gently open your eyes, feeling relaxed yet alert.

CHAPTER TEN

Your Citizenship

RESPECTING OTHERS AND YOUR ENVIRONMENT

When we condone or ignore lack of respect for other individuals we are bound to feel uneasy within ourselves at a deep level. When we respect ourselves we are more likely to respect other people and to respect our environment.

We live on a beautiful planet yet we seem constantly to abuse it. When we treat the planet with a lack of respect and a lack of consideration, it is really mirroring a lack of respect for ourselves. Now that some of the ways in which we damage the planet and the atmosphere have become public knowledge, it is important to do all we can to be respectful of the planet and for mankind's continued existence here. While it may be true that the planet could survive and adapt without us, we for the moment cannot live except on this one planet! Mankind has no other home.

So perhaps we should look more closely at our use of resources. How can we cut down on some of the things we use and on unwanted packaging? How can we make a positive contribution to preserving, protecting and nurturing aspects of the planet and life on it? Can we participate in the political process for the results that are now needed?

RESPECT FOR INDIVIDUALS

The rights of the individual in the law, respect for self, others and the environment, are tenets sadly missing in society today. The right of the individual to be treated with respect is fundamental. Without this we have an underlying problem in living together and working together. If you live in a city, or share a building with other people, you'll know some of the problems and challenges of living together peacefully with others. There are often disputes about the use of the garden, maintenance, cleaning of communally used areas, and – perhaps the biggest challenge of all – living with other people's noise. If you have ever been kept awake night after night with the steady boom of music from above, below or to the side of you, you'll be aware what an important area this is for personal freedom and self-esteem.

Always listen to your personal intuition, your hunches, and you will identify what it is important for *you* to do in every situation. As you take responsibility for your life, both as an individual and as a citizen, your self-esteem will rise, and you will find you have more energy to help others as well as yourself.

As I respect myself, I respect others and the environment.

YOU CAN MAKE A DIFFERENCE

There is much social and political change; the old order of things is changing and disappearing. At the same time as there are these changes, there are opportunities to participate, for there are many pressure groups where an individual can join with others. An important part of self-esteem building is believing in yourself and that you can make a difference. Whatever you have energy for with regard to the world, whether it's excitement about something being done, or anger at the way certain aspects of our life today are neglected, know that this surge of energy indicates the issue is important for you. Take notice. Be willing to formulate your ideas for positive change and take action.

While it is important that politicians listen to people and help them, it is also important that people speak up and make themselves heard, making clear what they need and want. This is at least the beginning of making politics a two-way process. From a point of self-esteem it is excellent to identify what you feel strongly about and do something about it. Now is the time to participate in what we might loosely call 'politics'. Your thoughts and actions could make the world a better place, promote peace, and ensure the survival of the planet.

You may have clear ideas of what is needed. Consciously hold pictures in your mind of clear waters and air, green trees and vegetation with people living together peacefully. You can discuss with like-minded people what the ideal solution to local and global problems may be. However, thoughts and words are *not* enough. Now is the time for action. So act responsibly and with self-esteem for our planet. We can act both individually and collectively to make a difference. There are many political, environmental and peace groups you can join. Look on the Internet or look out for information displayed locally.

I now make a difference by speaking out and taking action.

Focus on Peace

Especially at times when there is fear and panic, it is important to radiate harmonious thoughts and energy. At times of great fear, many people feel discomfort in the solar plexus area just below their rib cage. Rather than having your energy become harsher, defensive and aggressive, imagine pulling this energy up into your heart area to soften and transform it. We can help by clearing up any areas of lack of harmony within ourselves and with people in our own lives. From a point of peace within yourself, reflect on what is appropriate to say and to do.

I focus on peace and harmony for the world.

PERSONAL FOCUS

Making a Difference as a Citizen

1 What can you do as an individual in your daily life that will assist and support other people or the environment? Outline practical steps, beginning with one you can start right away.

2 Is there some larger cause that you feel passionately about, for example global peace or resolution of regional and global challenges? Is there some way you could be influential with others in holding out for appropriate action?

3 If you have a keen interest in decisions being made and passed as law, participate in the political process. Consider becoming a member of a political party, or a pressure group, e.g. to campaign for peace or for renewable energy instead of nuclear. Make a contribution in some way that is right for you.

RELAXATION

Respect For People and the Environment

Relax. Imagine yourself calm, serene, full of self-esteem. See yourself as healthy and radiant. Imagine yourself in perfect surroundings with clean water, sea, air and healthy vegetation. Imagine a world where people live peacefully, one country with another, one group with another.

SECTION FIVE

Your Body

CHAPTER ELEVEN

Self-Esteem and Your Body

SEE YOURSELF AS ATTRACTIVE

Do you like your body? Many people regard their body as unattractive. You may be spending a lot of time constantly bemoaning the fact that 'I'm unattractive, I'm overweight, my legs are too short' or whatever; this focuses your attention on what you don't like, not what you do like. You form a self-image of yourself as unattractive and that is what you project, broadcast out to the world. In addition, even when other people think you're fine you are liable to disbelieve them.

While you may decide it would be better for you to be lighter, fitter, to give some attention to your weight, hair or clothes, do so in a way that is as enjoyable as possible and gives you the results you want. Don't stop yourself doing things because you feel you're not attractive enough. Especially when you want to make changes, liking yourself is important – it is supportive and helpful. Don't wait until you have, for example, lost weight to start liking yourself and doing things you want to do! While your health and outer appearance will improve by nurturing, eating well and grooming, your appearance is also affected by your thoughts and feelings.

I focus on what is attractive about me.

There is much emphasis today on a person's outer image, yet how you think of and perceive yourself – your inner image – plays an important part in how others perceive you. So focus on the bits you like and you will find that these aspects are what others will notice.

Talk of your body as you'd like it to be – healthy and attractive. See your body that way in your mind's eye. When you hear yourself speaking or thinking about your body in a way that doesn't enhance your self-esteem, let go of that low-level way of perceiving yourself and see yourself as you'd like to be. What you focus on you get more of, so don't emphasize your flaws. Treat your body as a friend you want to love and support.

YOU ARE IN CONTROL OF YOUR BODY

You are probably already aware that you can be helpful or unhelpful to yourself with regard to food. You may be aware you are eating food compulsively to stuff your feelings and for comfort. If, as inevitably happens, you then feel guilty and worse afterwards, there is little enjoyment in the whole business. If you are eating lots of sweet things, see if you can find other ways to 'sweeten' your life by giving yourself more of the things you like.

Most compulsive behaviour adversely affects our bodies. We need to be committed enough to ourselves to want to change and move forward because doing so is better for our self-esteem and as such is more joyful for us. As soon as you hear yourself saying 'never again', you know that yes, you'll do it! What is needed is for you to forgive yourself for what you feel you have been doing wrong, stop blaming yourself. In all change, this is vital, and particularly so with behaviour you want to change.

Notice, too, what feelings you are ignoring or even keeping down by continuing the behaviour that you want to change – whether it's one of indulgence, neglect or procrastination. What is it you're really feeling? It is safe to feel your feelings.

As you do so they will become more comfortable and supportive. Is there a way you could be kinder to yourself? Are you listening to what you really want, both what your body wants and what you want for yourself in your life? Start giving yourself more of what you want. That also means taking the appropriate action to move forward with your life.

I am starting to give myself what I really want.

Are you thinking about going on a diet or an exercise programme to lose weight and shape up? Perhaps you've been on diets and exercise programmes before but have then slid back into old habits. Maybe you have got to where you wanted to be and then gone back with a crash to your former weight. Diet and exercise can help, but if your weight is really difficult to shift, in spite of appropriate diet and exercise, then mental and emotional factors can be considered.

First, perhaps you could ask 'What am I waiting for?' Is there some area of your life where you are wanting to move forward? If so, then make it a priority to identify what you want to achieve and see how you can do this. Are you holding yourself back with the dead weight of your own disappointed desires? You may be telling yourself you'll do *it* when you've lost weight, yet you may be hanging on to that weight simply because you're not moving ahead with what you'd love to do in your heart.

Fear and all our emotions can become very solid if we don't want to recognize them. Extra weight can be the way the body adapts to stress. Where there is a fear of being hurt, you may find you unconsciously add a layer to protect yourself. Try taking a deep breath and relaxing; just feel what you're feeling. Keep reminding yourself it is safe to feel your feelings, at all times. As you recognize and accept your feelings, you will find it easier to make the changes you want in your behaviour.

It is safe for me to feel my feelings.

HANDLING PAIN AND ILLNESS

When you're feeling low physically your priority must be to relax and take care of yourself. Do what you can to keep to or adapt arrangements with others, yet beyond a certain point don't push yourself. If you do, you'll achieve very little and make yourself far worse. Throughout any time of illness, look after your body, for behind many colds and 'flu bugs lies the exhaustion that makes us more susceptible to them. Very often we are too busy to identify and put in place what we need to keep us well – the rest, relaxation, helpful attitude, food, exercise, companionship and work that suits us best.

When you're physically ill it is particularly difficult to feel high self-esteem, to feel centred. There is a tendency to let your condition get you down. It is therefore doubly important to do all you can to help yourself. Do all you can to relieve any pain, whether it is by conventional or alternative medicine. If you can, try to listen to uplifting, soothing music. This is *not* the time to puzzle out why and how this has happened even if the problem is recurring or chronic. Remind yourself that the worst symptoms are temporary, envisage feeling better and more comfortable. As you lie comfortably, send messages to your cells to heal and function perfectly, bring in the memory of a time before your discomfort when you felt well and full of vitality. If you are in an uncomfortable state, ask yourself what thing, what small thing you can do that would give you joy. It may be listening to a particular programme on the radio, having a soothing bath, sitting propped up comfortably so that you can look through a favourite magazine. Listen to your personal intuition to revitalize yourself. Help yourself by visualizing yourself as whole, healthy and vibrant.

As I relax and rest my health is restored.

It can be worrying if someone close to you is ill, particularly if they seem to be getting worse, and especially if they seem unsettled in themselves. You will want to do all you can for them. But if you can do no more, constantly feel guilty or tired and feel your efforts are coming to nothing, then it is time to draw back your energy. You can always assist another person by having the thought that they're healed and whole. Speak in helpful, encouraging words to them. Boost their self-esteem and remind them of how well they are doing, how far they have come. Bring into the conversation times in the past when they've enjoyed good health and plenty of energy. Your demonstration of high self-esteem with compassionate goodwill will have an uplifting effect on them. Send healing thoughts at times you are not with them.

I send healing thoughts and love.

ADD ENERGY AND LIGHT TO YOUR BODY

Whatever your age or physical condition, you can play with energy and light to improve your vitality. It goes without saying that if you've been given good medical advice or are aware of steps you can take to help yourself, then do them! However, you can also get your body relaxed and imagine light moving through it to nurture and energize yourself. The idea of light is so easy to imagine that you can do this when you're lying in bed or sitting down relaxing. Picture or feel all the energy that runs through the body, flowing smoothly and harmoniously. You can also energize yourself by sitting for a short while in the sun with due care to sun protection – 5 minutes is enough. Feel or imagine the sun replenishing your life-force and energy. Think of yourself as strong, healthy and as full of energy as you'd like to he.

I add energy and light to my body.

WHAT IS BEST FOR *YOUR* BODY?

Each person, being unique, has special optimum requirements in all aspects of life. Ask yourself what would be the
most helpful thing you could do for your body right now?
Should you stop and relax, move about, eat particular foods
or have a massage? Just ask yourself and you'll find out! If
your body had a voice what would it be telling you right
now? Would it be, 'I'm exhausted, I want looking after?'
Listen and you'll get the answer! Then go into action in a
way that is enjoyable and energizing for you.

Low self-esteem thoughts and stress are real energy sap-
pers. A combination of fear and the thought that your
feelings are not important leads to a daily build-up of
anxiety and worry which causes exhaustion. Find out what
works for you and take practical steps. Remember that your
needs will change at different times.

Just as you are a unique, wonderful and special individual, so your body is unique and wonderful, with its own
special energies and changing needs and requirements. Listen to your personal intuition as to what your body needs
and wants. It will respond to your treating it well. Have your
habits and attitudes support you to keep your self-esteem
high and in having the energy to live life to the full.

*As I do what is best for my body, I have more and
more energy.*

PERSONAL FOCUS

What is Best for Your Body?

1 Relax, and then make up a programme of all the good
things you can do for your body over the next three months.

2 What is one good thing you can do for your body, starting
today?

3 Even while you're doing things that help you feel better, you can help yourself by remembering thoughts that add further energy, e.g. 'I'm strong and healthy', 'My body is healthy', 'I take time for myself', 'I support my body in all I do'. Add you own helpful thoughts to these.

RELAXATIONS

Looking After Your Body

In a relaxed state, ask your personal intuition what you can do with regard to your body. What would benefit and support it? If there is pain or tension, ask what you need to do to put yourself at ease.

Feeling at Ease and Energized

Follow your general relaxation. Now see yourself in your mind's eye sending extra love and support to any areas which are tense, uncomfortable or which you feel judgmental about with regard to appearance. Now dissolve that image and relax even more deeply, picture yourself with the extra energy and sense of relaxation you'd like for yourself. Notice how good you feel. Relax and hold that picture, then let it go totally, letting the good feelings stay with you.

Feeling at Ease and Energized

Follow your general relaxation. Now see yourself in your mind's eye sending extra love and support to any areas which are tense, uncomfortable or which you feel judgmental about with regard to appearance. Now dissolve that image and relax even more deeply, picture yourself with the extra energy and sense of relaxation you'd like for yourself. Notice how good you feel. Relax and hold that picture, then let it go totally, letting the good feelings stay with you.

SECTION SIX

Your Money

CHAPTER TWELVE

Self-Esteem and Your Money

MOVING THROUGH FINANCIAL DIFFICULTIES

It may be at this time that you're experiencing financial difficulties as many people are. Even if you're not having problems yourself, you'll probably know someone who is. This can range from having wage increases stopped or your house's value go down to losing everything on the material level – jobs, income and subsequently a home. There is fear and uncertainty around with regard to money.

If you're one of the many people who are experiencing financial difficulties, then take heart. It is not necessarily your fault, for the old rules simply don't apply any more. On the other hand, you may be finding all sorts of opportunities for making money that didn't seem to be around before. When old established ways are changing there can seem to be both far less money and far more.

When you don't have the money you feel you need, even to pay for essentials, it can be extremely worrying and frightening. If you're in this situation, and many people are today through no fault of their own, you may be feeling paralysed, unable to do anything or even to think straight and finding it difficult to concentrate at work or on finding a job. You may feel withdrawn. You'll probably be panicking as you imagine all the worst kinds of scenarios unfolding.

Another reaction you may have is to try and pretend the whole thing isn't happening, to blank it out by eating, drinking and sleeping too much or watching television excessively. If you're with another person, it may be that you're at the stage of pulling each other down by amplifying the worry, focusing on the problem rather than on any possible solutions.

I focus on solutions to this situation.

Now what you must hold to and believe in is that there is a solution, a way or ways that this can be resolved. Your initial and most important step is to believe this, especially when there's little sign of actual improvement. It's an act of faith which ties in with your self-esteem principles of holding out for better circumstances and situations even while your current situation seems bleak.

You need a way of handling the strain of the situation so you can get on with your life and be in a position to resolve this challenge. There are practical steps that will help. Remember that this is a *situation*; it needn't be an emotional drama even if it feels like one.

There are times when we feel like giving up completely, that nothing is working, that we've done everything wrong. This is where 'mental muscle', determination, and courage come in. You can make the decision to see things in a positive frame, because you always can, no matter what. Importantly, at the same time, look at and be willing to take your best course of action.

Taking action diminishes my fear and anxiety.

There is an ebb and flow in most situations in life. When you are broke this is the ebb tide with regard to money. You'll handle the challenges this brings if you can find a way of keeping relaxed yet alert with regard to the situation. It's important to remember that your self-value and self-worth are still there, regardless of your situation. Stop blaming yourself or others for what has happened. That is not to say you are not going to ask for the necessary reparations, for bills to be paid to you, money owing to come in. See what can you do today that will help the situation. First of all, with regard to communicating with those you owe money to, small regular payments may be acceptable. What can you do today with regard to creating or receiving more money? What practical steps can you take, however small?

CREATING MORE MONEY

Contrary to what you may have been told, wanting and asking for more money is a good thing! Establish for yourself the new thought 'I want more money', 'I deserve more money'. We're told all sorts of things about money which can be very unhelpful, that 'money won't make you happy', 'it can't buy you love', 'is the root of all evil' and 'doesn't grow on trees'.

Although money is often equated with status and worth, your true worth and value is constant and independent of your finances. It is best for you to have your money serve you, so that you can do what is useful and enjoyable for yourself and others. Limiting thoughts and fears, old ways of thinking, can restrict your ability to receive money, to enjoy it, and to use it in ways that are beneficial. Let go of those thoughts or change them, literally trade them in for some more helpful thoughts! Restrictions in other areas of your life may also inhibit the flow of money to you. So if you're unwell, doing work that you dislike or that you know is no longer appropriate for you, or if you're miserable in one or more of your relationships, you may find you become closed down and protective and this will affect your capacity and ability to receive.

I remember my true worth.

From a point of high self-esteem, be creative, think of all the ways money could come to you – not just the way or ways you now receive it. There will be many ways money will flow to you perhaps by selling a product you have found beneficial. You may win something – pools, competitions, the lottery, premium bonds – but you need to enter first! Open yourself to new and different ways of money coming in.

Sometimes, because you are feeling low or worried, you will accept offers of money or opportunities to create money in an ungracious way. Without gratitude it can seem to others that you are not that worried or that the offer is not wanted or appreciated. It is important not to diminish opportunities to receive money, but to create new ones, so take care to communicate your appreciation and gratitude. Saying thank you is always helpful – and you can always give back in other ways if you wish.

From a point of high self-esteem, think about how much more money you want. It can be helpful to have a specific amount in mind, be it a lump sum or a regular amount.

Remember, no amount of money will automatically give you security or self-esteem. You must develop from within. Developing self-esteem and a sense of inner security first will make it easier to move more confidently into increased income and you can feel good right away. With self-esteem you don't need to wait until some particular conditions are fulfilled to feel good about yourself and your life.

I experience high self-esteem whatever my financial situation.

YOUR PURPOSE FOR YOUR MONEY

Consider what you would do with increased income. What purpose would it serve? What use do you have for more money? It may be to save and invest or to spend on some specific items, personal or linked with business. It may be linked with your development, courses you want to take, learning personal or specific skills linked to your work. Write out your list. Have firm goals, perhaps within a set time frame, getting all the practical advice on finances you need from independent advisors. If you have any last doubts about whether you deserve the money, whether you'll use it well, clear them now. You do deserve more money and you always have deserved money. You are now open to receiving it. Notice in reality how having more money would assist you, how it would benefit you. Be aware also of the benefits to others if you have more money available.

LISTEN TO YOUR PERSONAL INTUITION

When you get into the habit of relaxing and listening to your intuition, you will become more aware of all sorts of hints, suggestions, flashes of inspiration, over what to do next. Write down what these suggestions are. See if you can take practical action. Remember, your personal intuition over money matters, as over other aspects of your life, will come out with suggestions that may seem small, even ordinary, and yet provide an important key to moving forward with your finances.

Trust your intuition as to the level of security you want. Put that in your plans and goals for money. Clarity about the amount of money you want and your purpose for your money is important to put in place. Listening to your intuition you will learn how you can best use your money to benefit yourself and others in line with your new increased self-esteem and the expectations that that quite rightly brings.

My having more money benefits me and others.

Having Extra Money

Especially when you feel you're moving out of 'survival' it is appropriate for your self-esteem to have your money support you and work for you. You will probably want maximum flexibility in the use of your money in the present with long-term security. Clarity is required here so you keep your outgoings well below your income. When you raise the level of your income it is easy to have your outgoings rise, getting everything bigger and better, so you're no better off in terms of extra cash.

It needn't become a time-consuming obsession, yet make it a priority to find out all you can about the best ways to manage your money and get the optimum yield. If one of your aims is financial security and independence, work out what money you would want or need for that and see how you can work towards this. Realize you deserve this financial abundance which will enrich your life and the lives of others.

I am grateful for the wealth and richness in my life.

Personal Focus

Handling Financial Difficulties

1 The first step is to believe in yourself, that there is a way through this situation and that you can resolve it. It is very important to believe that, to have faith. You can help yourself by changing all your thoughts to helpful ones. Write these down.

2 Make a list of all those to whom you owe money and the amounts. Consciously let go of blaming yourself for this; you'll resolve the situation sooner than you think. Now work out who you can afford to pay even a small amount.

Start with essentials like mortgage, rent and utilities. Don't over-estimate the amounts you can pay and then judge yourself for not being able to keep payments up. If you find this difficult to do because it's upsetting, get a friend you trust to help you – someone who will do this in quite a detached way. You don't need to have a financial advisor.

Remember, it is essential to explain your situation to those to whom you owe money and to give them a realistic idea of when, and how much, you can pay (small regular amounts may be acceptable).

3 Project that you *will* have this money. Work out all the things you can do to bring money in, starting with something today.

4 Make sure you enjoy other areas of your life for there are still many things you can enjoy and experience. You may become more aware of these areas. Be open to your personal intuition as to the best way ahead. There will be pointers for the present and the future, new opportunities or the spur to a new way of doing things may come from this.

Receiving More Money

1 Write down the increased amount of money you want. This may be a lump sum, an annual or a monthly amount. You can adjust the sum as appropriate, particularly after you've looked at exercise 2 below.

2 What do you want the money for? Now make a list of your needs and the amounts you imagine you might need for them. At this point don't try to work out how this may come to you.

3 What are the ways money could come to you? As you relax, what suggestions are you receiving? What is it you need to do? What can you put into practice? Are there any other ways that what you want may come to you? Write this all down.

4 Write down what you will now do.

Increased Wealth

1 Write out a description of your improved situation, filling in the detail. Check, then add anything you may have left out.

2 Write out new financial goals for your increased amounts.

3 Assisted by your personal intuition as in the relaxation, be open to new opportunities. Write down any hints or insights as they occur, regarding steps to take, people to contact, and then take immediate action. Include in your practical steps all that you want to do and to give yourself, money available right now and also for the future.

4 Importantly, continue to 'think' and 'feel' rich, being grateful for your wealth. Bring in feelings of security and success. Express your gratitude.

RELAXATIONS

Attracting the Money You Want

Get yourself as relaxed as you can with your body placed comfortably, your breathing normal and relaxed. Now imagine a beautiful scene that you know or can imagine, where you feel a sense of safety. Bring in a sense of courage, a sense of inner security, a sense of trust that you will come through this. Call on your courage and listen to your personal intuition on what it is appropriate for you to do.

Let go of your old, negative, limiting thoughts and allow new, helpful thoughts to take their place. What are some of these? Allow them in and feel that you now deserve greater financial security, you now have money flowing to you. You have sufficient money coming in – more than enough money to meet essentials and also to make other plans.

Listen to your personal intuition. Are there any other insights that would be helpful to you? Come slowly out of your relaxation and record what you will now do and when you will do this.

Experiencing Increased Wealth

In particular see how this is beneficial to yourself and others! With your new increased wealth, imagine what a particular day will be like: just picture it, see what you're doing, what sorts of people you're with, what kind of surroundings you're in. Notice how well and happy you look and how assured and accomplished you feel, or whatever good feelings you imagine you'd have in such circumstances. Fill in the details: the better you can imagine it, the better it will turn out to be. Using your personal intuition see if there are suggestions as to what it would help you to know or to do. Any answers will come either now or later: you may continue to have hints, whispers and suggestions. When you come out of the relaxation, note down any ideas or practical steps that now occur to you.

SECTION SEVEN

Self-Esteem and Your Work

CHAPTER THIRTEEN

Your Job and Changes at Work

Your Job and Your Self-Esteem

It is essential for your self-esteem and well-being that you find work that you enjoy, work that fills you with energy and enthusiasm while you are doing it. You need to be able to see the results of your work and the contribution that you are making. This is important not only because of the amount of time you spend at work but also because there is a deep relationship between your self-esteem, your well-being and the work you do.

You may think this is all very well but doesn't apply to you, if you are in the position of not being able to get any work whatsoever at the moment. However, it depends on your perspective. It can feel difficult when you've either got no work or you are in a job you hate. Yet the more you can see an optimistic picture of the wider view, the more you can help yourself. Remember that what you bring to any job or project you are working on is very special, going far beyond any job title. You are unique and special regardless of your job status or job description.

Almost any job of work can be done in a way that enhances your self-esteem. This is of course also excellent for the person or people you're working with and for. It is also energizing and more satisfying than doing things in a half-hearted manner. Even if you're not sure you are in the right job or you want to change jobs, for your own well-being do things wholeheartedly while you are there. Very often you can feel low in a job just before it's time for a change, but you can work out in your free time what you really want to be doing.

I have a unique contribution to make.

THE CHANGING WORLD OF WORK

You may have been experiencing great upheavals at work and in your expectations about a job. The old world of work where you joined an organization and stayed for life or for many years is fast becoming a thing of the past. As companies streamline and use outside agencies more and more, people are finding themselves being made redundant, being re-deployed, being put on short-term contracts, opting for a second career or going self-employed.

As work and money are so closely linked for most people, you can feel a double threat to your security. You may have done all the appropriate things yet still find yourself in a worrying situation through no fault of your own. Particularly at times of structural and financial change fear can predominate. Many people are feeling insecure and scared at work and this is leading to behaviour which often seems unacceptable, such as bullying and putting the blame onto other people. Managers and those in authority do have a particular duty to manage their own energy well, to integrate their own emotions of fear, anger and helplessness so that they can help others to do the same. Experience your emotions at home, in private, and let them change. However bad the situation, it is essential to relax, trust and take a positive view. By all means plan ahead with alternative strategies for the future, but also see what you can do to progress the situation today. Ensure that you have moments that are pleasant and joyful – say a walk through the park, a relaxing bath or talking to a supportive friend. As you overview your day, see how you can, for example, get through what you need to do in a way that doesn't feel pressured. This is the time to counter stress and do things in a way that suits you.

On the one hand there is an erosion of security, yet on the other hand there is the opportunity to build the only real security there is, that comes from within. For many people this changing of the old rules can seem like a welcome reprieve from the old world of work, where things have felt static and inflexible. They have been tied for too long. There are more ideas around about new ways of working and with them many more opportunities.

My true security comes from me.

FINDING WORK THAT IS RIGHT FOR YOU

When you do work that is right for you, using your unique talents and abilities, you feel joyful and confident and know that you are giving an excellent service. Doing work you love is one of the best things for your self-esteem. It is doubtful whether you can experience consistently high self-esteem if you're not in work that is right for you. The clues to what you most want to do come from seeing things in the outer world that you'd love to do and even more by looking within, noticing the things that energize you and that you enjoy. So listen to your personal intuition: through hints, nudges, whispers, daydreams or dreams, you will get clues that you can build into a fuller picture. When you think about things you'd love to do or daydream about doing things, write them down, then see what practical steps you need to take to achieve them.

It is important that you do what is right for you with regard to work not only from the perspective of feeling fulfilled and experiencing high self-esteem but also from the angle of your contribution to the world. When we do the work that is right for us we always make a contribution. We make the world a better place, whether that be for the people immediately around us or for a wider section of the population.

It's not always essential to change your job when things aren't going well. It may be feasible to make changes to and add new facets to the job you are currently doing. If the problem is a relationship with a colleague, resolving this may make all the difference so that you can focus your energy and attention to move forward. However, if you have done all in your power to resolve the problem and you still do not feel satisfied, especially if this continues over a period of time, then it is important to look at alternatives. While you may need to work towards this by training or gaining experience it can be useful to visualize, to daydream about what you'd absolutely love to be doing and notice what the essential elements for you are.

I listen to my personal intuition on the best work for me.

What are these elements that are important to you? How could you move nearer to doing them? If there's something you have a lot of energy for, or a passionate interest in, whether you feel pleased to see things are going well or feel angry at the way things are being done, pay attention to your feelings. This may be with regard to something in your local area or far away but brought into your house nightly on your television screen. Notice which aspects concern you most, for example intimidation, lack of care for the environment, or inappropriate use of finances. Sometimes it's possible to get a job in your area relevant to your concern or interest, for example with a charity.

It isn't however always necessary or even desirable to change jobs in order to 'help the world'. Staff from a large company we work with in central London were concerned about the welfare of other people who were homeless. They organized themselves to help a local organization once a month to provide food and clothing. They are also now campaigning for more attention to be given to finding a solution. When there is something you feel passionately about, you can often find a local group who are actively working for improvements and who would welcome your contribution, your time and skills, even one evening or afternoon a month.

I now know what I can do to help myself and others.

PERSONAL FOCUS

In Your Current Job

Regardless of your current job situation just note the following down:

1 What is satisfying about your current job? Could you expand this aspect of it?

2 What aspects of your current work do you find unsatisfactory? Are there any ways you can improve on them?

3 What else in your current work situation can you do to improve your work or add to it? Write down these things and decide to take action. What can you do today?

4 Which people can you speak to in enlisting help or support if necessary?

5 Is there anyone at work whom you could express your

appreciation or give additional support to? Decide that you will do this.

6 Is there some way you could spend a small amount of time doing voluntary work or creative work that you are drawn to?

7 What are the most self-esteem-enhancing thoughts that you can have? Write these down and repeat them to yourself. For example, 'I am becoming more and more successful', 'I am making a valuable contribution', 'I am worthy', 'I am worthwhile'.

Changes at Work

1 What change or changes are you experiencing at work? Write them down as a situation not an emotional drama.

Now write down your feelings on this situation. If these feelings involve blaming yourself or another person, let go of these, and of course you can turn up your feelings of joy and enthusiasm.

2 What are the real sources of security in your life? For example, your connection with your personal intuition and from those close to you? Notice how you can rely on these.

As you focus more on feeling secure and centred you will experience this more and more. Decide you will have peace of mind right now.

RELAXATIONS

Harmony At Work

See yourself at work in a harmonious co-operative atmosphere; notice all that is going well. There is trust and co-operation. See if you can give and receive support. Using your personal intuition, see where you can improve your service. Be aware of what you can do and need to know.

Moving Through Change

As you relax, see yourself moving comfortably through change; from a position of confidence see yourself viewing the situation as something you can act upon. Listening to your personal intuition, ask if there is anything you can do to help the situation or if there is a higher view you can take of it. When you come out of the relaxation you can write this down and continue to be in touch with this inspiration from your intuition.

CHAPTER FOURTEEN

Dealing with Redundancy and Unemployment

THE EXPERIENCE OF REDUNDANCY

If redundancy hits you personally it will come as a shock, despite the fact that more and more people are finding themselves being made redundant, being re-deployed or put on short-term contracts. While this is commonplace today it is still upsetting when you find yourself in this situation. You may be told it's nothing to do with you personally, economic cuts are needed, yet it's difficult not to take things personally, especially when you've worked for an organization for a long time. You may be feeling low and worried about your future as well as experiencing a drop in your self-esteem. It's usual in the circumstances to question your value and worth. You may be experiencing self-doubt and feel the organization has a really low opinion of you to do such a thing. This can affect your opinion of yourself, so it's important to remind yourself immediately that whatever you're feeling, your value and worth remain intact. Your true value is not dependent on your current career or financial status.

I remember I am of great value whatever my work situation.

REDUCE YOUR STRESS

Imposed change, such as redundancy and re-deployment, can cause stressful reactions within us and the ongoing uncertainty and fear generated needs to be countered by measures to reduce stress at physical, mental and emotional levels. Self-esteem work is essential in reducing stress, especially in preparations for interviews and job decisions, as well as keeping motivated on a daily basis. In particular be persistent in changing dominant unhelpful thought patterns and therefore in reinforcing a supportive way of thinking. So when you have unstructured time you may also feel anger and resentment about your redundancy. You need to learn to integrate these emotions and harness the power from them. This is an important part of coming to terms with redundancy. Learn to recognize your emotions. Accept and experience them. Troublesome emotions will then shift, causing less stress and exhaustion than would occur if you either suppressed them or expressed them inappropriately. It's common in times of uncertainty to feel others do not understand or support you, whether or not this really is the case. Above all, let go of resentment. It is particularly important to treat others with respect and encouragement when you may be feeling fraught. Let go of judgements so you can more easily move on.

I am patient with myself and others.

To help you feel less tense, learn the steps to practical relaxation and do some daily. To your relaxation programme add a moderate amount of exercise, as well as eating foods that are nutritious and suit your individual metabolism. Get practical advice if you're worried about money – for example, the Citizens Advice Bureau now has various forms of financial counselling. Don't be afraid to ask for support from family and friends or advice from professionals. Remember that each area of your life affects the other areas. Check the emphasis you're giving to every area of your life, for example, your body, family, friends, hobby and time for yourself. It is so important at this time to maintain balance in your life and look after yourself. The best you is always an unstressed you.

ESTABLISH A SENSE OF PURPOSE

It is also essential to have a sense of purpose – your personal statement on what you see as your overall aims and values for your working life. You need this sense of purpose to apply to and monitor your daily activities. You can revise and refine this, but keep it as your daily reminder. Notice what qualities you have – for example, courage, determination, creativity – that will ensure you of success. Focus your attention on goals that are in line with your purpose and that you are enthusiastic about achieving. Outline both long-term and short-term goals with practical steps to be taken.

NETWORKING AS PART OF YOUR JOB SEARCH

As well as friends, family, social contacts and former colleagues knowing you are looking for the right job, it's helpful to get out to places where there are 'employers'. Job fairs can be useful, but make sure they cover the area that you're interested in. Conferences, seminars, business people's clubs, perhaps the Chamber of Commerce can also help. You may need to join some of these, so have simple business cards printed with your name, address and telephone number. You needn't specify what you do, but it does oil the social business wheels if you have a card to give out. If you're at home or in a re-deployment department you also need to get out and about as well as checking the newspapers daily and the specialist magazines as they come out. There will be other ways you can get jobs and you need to pursue these by networking with people you meet. Write to firms expressing your interest and follow up with a phonecall. Get the name of the person you need to contact from the switchboard before you write. With people you meet remember that if you seem upbeat instead of worried and anxious, they are more likely to envisage you in a job and be more helpful in suggesting contacts.

I am open to new opportunities.

MAINTAINING YOUR MOTIVATION

There is definitely a way ahead for more exciting and fulfilling opportunities. Just have faith in yourself and your ability to succeed, and realize that you do have a purpose. It takes courage and patience to go through changes and challenging times. There is work and a way of working that is special to you and you will find out what this is. Remember to treat yourself gently yet be determined to succeed.

It is essential to value yourself when you are going through the process of re-deployment or redundancy. It is so easy to undervalue yourself. The truth is that you are of great value regardless of your current job status and you have many unique qualities and abilities. Be aware of the value of what you have to offer: this is a constant – it hasn't changed just because of your changing job situation. This belief in yourself constitutes your 'inner CV' and is as vital at any interview you may be going to as anything you have down on paper. Building a stronger belief in yourself has great practical benefits, both with regard to how you handle this time of change and to the results you get.

I believe in myself.

MOVING INTO EMPLOYMENT

If you've been unemployed long-term, or as is the case with many young people who have never had a job, it is important to build your self-esteem and to examine what you truly want to be doing and then go for it.

One thing you will have is time, and although it can feel like your enemy it can also be your friend. Certainly you will need courage to combat the negative aspects of being out of work or never having had a job. You already have the courage and the interest in that you are reading this book. So now work out what you really want to do, what appeals to you. Could you start to do that now or could you get the necessary training? Is it feasible to move to an area where you can do this work?

See if you can conceive of a purpose for yourself. Do you have some sense of direction to guide you as to what you really want to do? What do you dream of doing? What are your flashes of inspiration, hints, hunches? Write them down, see what you can do on a daily basis to move towards your goal. Have your long-term goals but also work out what you want to do each week, each day even. For example, you could make three phonecalls, write two letters, put down the wording for a new slant to your CV. Never give up.

You may change your ideas of what you want for yourself, but never give up on yourself. You deserve to have well-paid work you enjoy doing. Look at all the practicalities. Is there a job you could do meanwhile that would give you the money you need to live on, yet which would mean you have time and energy to do some sort of training or voluntary work that will progress you towards, your final aim?

You will need determination, especially if you're around people who are in the same situation, that is without a job, and who are being negative about it. Do what you can to ensure that you don't get pulled down. Seek out positive company, those who support you and whom you can also support in being positive and upbeat. Never underestimate the power of the inner work and the practical steps you are taking. You can develop a courage, strength and belief in yourself that will be invaluable to you as you move into the paid position you are looking for.

My courage and determination bring me success.

Personal Focus

Opportunity Through Redundancy/Unemployment

1 For your 'inner CV' list all your good qualities, abilities and achievements, whether or not you used them in your last job. Note particularly those that you enjoy. Include personal qualities.

2 On a daily basis, choose thoughts that are helpful; keep approving of yourself. Now write down some of these helpful approving thoughts.

3 You may be blaming yourself or someone else, for example your last boss, for your present situation. Get this out of your system by writing out all you feel they have done 'wrong', then claim back your energy and attention by deciding to stop blaming. Write out 'I now choose to stop blaming, I move forward with energy and enthusiasm'.

4 Look after yourself. You are your most valuable asset. Combat stress and keep your lifestyle in balance. What can you do towards this?

5 Outline your 'purpose' and the perfect job description for you. Then you can look for actual jobs – or plan to set up your own business – in line with this.

6 What exhibitions, professional societies, seminars can you attend to get you out making contacts? Have a business card ready to take with you.

7 Write out your long-term and short-term goals.

8 On a daily basis you need variety. Write out what you can do without strain, eg three phonecalls, one letter, checking the papers and journals, as well as attending an interview, a meeting or a visit.

RELAXATION

Creating Opportunity

Go through your relaxation procedure, relaxing your body, getting comfortable, your breathing normal but relaxed, and going to your place of beauty and calm. Feel yourself drawing work to you, the right work for you at the right pay. Imagine yourself in a job you'd love to do, confident and enthusiastic, using your skills and special qualities. Imagine what that job would look like and feel like. Just picture it. Feel yourself drawing the right people and situations to you. Listen to your personal intuition regarding what it is best for you to do. Remain open to these suggestions as you go about your daily life, then write them down and act on them as appropriate. Now gently open your eyes.

CHAPTER FIFTEEN

Being Successfully Self-Employed

In the new world of work with cut-backs and more pressures than before, what was once thought of as being insecure – that is working for yourself – can in fact provide you with greater security. By being responsible for yourself, for your present and your future, you have little or no dependency on the whims of others and their changing energies.

To be self-employed and run your own small business successfully you need to have high self-esteem, a strong belief in yourself and what you're doing. You need enthusiasm, energy, and good business knowledge or advice on the financial side. Above all, both from the financial angle and for your personal satisfaction, you need to love the work you do. There is an abundance of advice available through government training schemes, free or at a low cost, regarding self-employment so do take advantage of these. However, one of the most practical things you can learn to do, one which is rarely taught on these courses, is to learn to listen to your intuition. Your personal intuition can be a valuable source of guidance and inspiration, for example on how and when to start up your business and develop it.

I listen to my personal intuition for the right steps to take.

LOOKING AFTER YOURSELF

Remember, you are your most valuable asset and it's vital that you keep yourself well, meaning not just free from illness but in the peak of health with an abundance of energy. Do what you need to keep yourself fit and build that into your daily routine as a matter of course. This will include attention to what you eat. Don't let stress build up but tackle it on a daily basis. A few minutes' relaxation, a short walk, catching yourself before you get tense, these all help. You'll be able to manage your business much better if you look after yourself.

I look after myself – I am my most valuable asset.

BUILDING YOUR BUSINESS

If you're newly self-employed and have been used to being in a 9.00-to-5.00 job you may find all sorts of bewildering emotions popping up, and it's important to acknowledge these feelings so you can integrate them and focus on your business. If you hit difficulties it is important to stop blaming yourself and others, let go quickly, learn the lesson you need to and move on. People you choose as associates and colleagues need to be positive and to share the same vision as you although they are likely to have different skills and abilities and areas of expertise. Most of all you need to be able to trust them. Build the financial aspect into your long-term and short-term goals. If you start to panic about money, tap into the quality of courage you already possess to be self-employed in the first place. Look at what steps you can take today to bring in money and to improve your business.

Make sure that the purpose of your work is so exciting and enjoyable for you, and so valuable to others, that nothing can stop you. Being self-employed you literally cannot afford not to have some quiet time with yourself, to listen to your personal intuition regularly, to look at your next business steps. You'll save time and money and energy by doing this, rather than rushing ahead. Then of course you need to put your plans into action with confidence.

I am attracting the right colleagues, associates and customers.

HAVING BALANCE IN YOUR LIFE

Self-employed people are more liable to work long hours and, particularly when a business is run from home, there can be an overflow into all hours of the day. When you consciously choose to do this that's fine and it's sometimes necessary to get the job done, but don't just let it happen. Above all, watch your health and keep your energy high; having a day off is essential and important, as is being with friends and family. A couple of nights away or a week may work well – then you don't have excessive preparation before leaving the business or heaps to catch up with on your return. More than anything you need to learn to relax as a priority daily.

KEEP YOUR SELF-ESTEEM HIGH FOR SUCCESS

Self-esteem is essential for self-employed people for sustained self-motivation as well as for selling products and services. Particularly at times when it feels difficult to remain self-motivated, come back to your core beliefs about yourself. It's important to remember you bring your unique qualities to the work you do. Remember too what is special about what you have to offer.

I am confident and successful.

PERSONAL FOCUS

1 Write out your business plan for the next five years. What do you want to achieve in terms of business and sales? How many people do you want to work with and for? Be sure to include the financial aspect, making clear what is net, gross and clear profit. You can adjust this as appropriate, as various aspects change. Keep a notebook for this or use your computer.

2 Write out your goals, your plans, for the next three months, month by month, then week by week, revising them as the time approaches. Remember to build in the amount of money you want to be receiving. You need short-term as well as long-term goals. Record this in your notebook.

3 Is there any single step you can take today to bring in more money? For example, are there satisfied customers you can ask for referrals or can you contact the press regarding your services?

4 If you were one of your customers, what improvements would you like to see? Ask yourself this and then act upon what you learn.

5 Once again, write out your purpose, the bigger picture of why you're doing what you do. What do you want to achieve? How does what you're doing today tie in with your purpose?

6 Remind yourself of your motivation. Why do you want to succeed for yourself? What are the benefits to you personally and to others?

7 With regard to looking after your health, write down what you could do this week that would be beneficial to you with regard to relaxation, food you're eating and any gentle exercise you may want to take. Look at what you can do that will boost your energy.

8 What can you do that would keep your lifestyle in balance, eg other people that you love to see, something creative that you'd love to do? What are the opportunities there for you?

RELAXATION

Relax your body. To relax further, see yourself in a beautiful place that you know or can imagine, perhaps by the river or the sea. Then come back to see yourself in your mind's eye looking good and feeling successful, being in touch with your personal intuition. See yourself now in your business and imagine increasing that business. Picture this happening smoothly and easily in a way you can handle and also giving you the money that you want, keeping your lifestyle balanced. Send out lines of goodwill to smooth your way ahead. From your personal intuition check if there is anything in particular that it's appropriate that you know or do. When you come out of this relaxation, write down your goals and anything else you want to remember. Identify your practical steps and take action.

CHAPTER SIXTEEN

Your Purpose – the Right Work for You

Establishing what you really want to achieve is one of the most important and worthwhile things you can do for yourself. You may as you progress redefine and refine, spending time clarifying your objectives before you outline your goals and practical steps. You need to be persistent and patient; you may need to acquire skills, training, work and life experience to assist your evolving purpose.

It's never appropriate to compare yourself with another person, even one who has the same job title. You are unique. What you have to offer is unique, both in your long-term plans and in how you use your time daily.

Unless you decide to look at what is important to you regarding what you want to achieve in your life, you may experience stress and those you're with will also experience your stress. Having talent and ability is not enough. Being able to focus on externals is not enough: you need to look within. Let your personal intuition assist you in finding a suitable vehicle for your many talents and abilities. You can identify these by noticing what you're good at, what gives you joy. To recognize those activities that give you fulfilment, that make you feel fully alive and at peace, you need time for yourself. When you're doing work you love – whether it be creating harmony among people, the ability to organize ideas or something else – you feel great and you nearly always excel at it.

When I am doing work I love, I do it well.

While career counselling and psychometric testing to assess your suitability for different jobs have their place, it's important for you as an individual to identify a purpose for yourself. When you're beginning to search for a job or moving from one job to another, listen to your personal intuition. This may give you clues as to what is best and right for you. Listen to yourself, to those whispers and hints from your personal intuition. Then take appropriate action.

When you're not putting your time and attention on what is best, then you tend to become unhappy, to look to other people and outside success to make you feel better. While we all need company, loving relationships, friends and family, no one else's advice can replace the promptings of your personal intuition. When you put your energy and attention where it needs to be you are at your best.

Purpose will vary from individual to individual. It may be that one person will publicly influence and assist many people, while another may not be known to those outside a small circle of friends and family. What is right for one person may not be appropriate for another. You gain access to your individual purpose through your personal intuition. It is by its nature unique and special to you just as you are unique and special.

My purpose is unique to me.

Having a sense of purpose is having a wider aim for yourself in your working life which will include, but go beyond, your current work situation. This will both give you a clear perspective on the way ahead and act to keep everything in balance. It is also a great booster and motivator and a reminder of your true value on days when you are feeling low and uninspired. As you listen to and use your personal intuition to shape your purpose for yourself and to adjust it, you will gain insight on your current situation and on the way ahead.

PERSONAL FOCUS

Establishing Your Purpose

1 Review your good qualities and abilities and note down which particular ones you enjoy.

2 Notice what is of importance as you look around the world as you see it. Are there certain things that you feel angry about or pleased about? You can look for ways in which you can contribute to them or help make changes.

3 What do you feel you have learned from facing challenges in your life? How could this help others? What have you really wanted and striven successfully to achieve?

4 Listen to your personal intuition for what it is best for you to do. When you relax in your dreams or daydreams, what can you imagine doing? Can you see any way in which these thoughts could be integrated into your current job or into starting your own business? Keep a note of your ideas and inspiration so that you can move forward.

5 As far as you can, define what you want to be doing, the essence of what you want to do, and write that down. Is there anything that would get you started in this: applying for a job, starting up on your own, taking some relevant training, doing some voluntary work? What practical steps can you take?

RELAXATION

The Right Work For You

Go through your relaxation procedure, relaxing your body, getting it comfortable, your breathing normal but relaxed, and imagining a place of beauty and calm. When you are really relaxed, see yourself in a job you'd love to do, confident and enthusiastic, using your skills and abilities. Imagine what that job would look like and feel like. Just picture it. Add anything you would want to make it as you'd like it to be. Now ask your personal intuition what it is best for you to do. Remain open to these hints and hunches as you go about your daily life. You can write them down and act on them as appropriate.

SECTION EIGHT

Review and Forward Focus

CHAPTER SEVENTEEN

Move Forward With Self-Esteem

Now that you have worked through this book and experienced benefits, it is so important to keep going. Even while you're aiming to make improvements you can do so in a relaxed way which feels enjoyable. The whole object is for you to feel better about yourself, more relaxed and energized. Be determined to have the life you want for yourself and prepared to take the necessary action to achieve it.

As the one certainty in life is change, having the means to build and maintain your self-esteem, as well as developing the habit of listening to your personal intuition, is your best insurance for your future. Believing in yourself and valuing yourself are vital. Inner security comes from kowingou can handle changes however unexpected and rapid. It comes from knowing you can trust your personal intuition when you listen to it regularly on what is best for you and your life. Just as a secure future comes from inner security and self-esteem, an exciting and fulfilling future comes from knowing that you already have the means to build and maintain your self-esteem so you can put your attention on yourself, the people in your life and what is important to you. Remember, it's never too late or too soon to create for yourself the life you want!

On a daily basis you can take steps to raise your level of self-esteem and self-confidence for better results in all areas of your life. Then there are various things you'll want to do each week and each month, after listening to your personal intuition to set goals that suit you. Improvements can be on a gradual basis and the benefits subtle, sometimes impercept-ible, until you realize how much your life has changed. For some people, outward appearances change dramatically, while for others they just feel better about themselves and their lives.

When things start to go well for you, when money, friendship, work and love start to come easily, you may begin to feel guilty. You may feel that something is now sure to go wrong; that you have to work extra hard so that things go well and if you do not that is somehow cheating! You may even subconsciously feel that if you do not struggle and suffer for results you haven't earned them – that you are not good enough within yourself to have what you want. These thoughts, as you'll realize by now, are unhelpful to your self-esteem, fulfilment and success in life. However, you now know how you can let go of or change around these thoughts and work with the various processes that have been outlined to set you on course for greater self-esteem.

Reports back from students show that putting the simple practices outlined above into daily use are beneficial. It helps to continually encourage yourself. One woman told us she had boosters up on a card in her kitchen and reminded herself of them daily. When we met she was moving through divorce and job loss. Over a period of one year, she emerged from the pain and upset stronger, calmer and more determined. And with both a better job and a better relationship! Below are some boosters which will help you.

SELF-ESTEEM BOOSTERS

- On a daily basis, stop criticizing yourself.
- Practise the three As of self-esteem building:

Appreciate yourself
Accept yourself
Approve of yourself

- Notice thoughts that are unhelpful:

'I will never get this done'
'I cannot handle this/him/her'
'I am not good enough'
  and change them to
'I am getting everything done'
'I can handle this'
'I am more than good enough'.
You will feel better as you keep repeating your new helpful thoughts, and you will get better results too!

- Add good feelings to your self-esteem thoughts so that you immediately feel confident and successful.

- Imagine putting repetitive worries about the future and the past into a box and see them disappearing from your mind. Then you will feel free to take any action that is appropriate. Have all your emotions acceptable. Relax and feel your feelings – they will change and become more comfortable.

- Stop blaming yourself and others. Revise the 'Free yourself from Blaming' process (page 37) whenever you want to. Move on to what is important to you and to doing what you enjoy. This will bring peace of mind.

- When faced with unexpected changes, relax and trust yourself to cope. Then you can more easily see what you need to do.

- Look for ways you can treat yourself better. Especially when you are under pressure, be extra kind to yourself and do things you enjoy.

- Relax for a few minutes daily. Listen to your personal intuition. You can ask yourself about any situation, 'What do I need to know? What do I need to do?' The answers will come either now or later. Listen to your personal intuition to guide you in what is best for you throughout the day.

- You are important, what you want is important. Where are you going? Dream, visualize, clarify. Listen to your personal intuition to set goals in easy stages and take action.

- Always remember, you *are* special, your life is precious!

BALANCE AND FOCUS IN YOUR LIFE

You may be aware that there is an area of your life that you need to put your attention on. It may be glaringly obvious; it may be more subtle – a feeling, say, of dissatisfaction or wanting more in a particular area. If you are unsure, check the balance in your life, noticing how you'd like each area to be. Now choose one area to work on first with some goal-setting. It is very important to write down what you want. After all, you do this when you go to the supermarket, so it's even more important for what you want in your life!

In your boosters you'll notice that you are reminded that you are important! What you want is important. Only you can decide what you want. This is an ongoing process. It means you need to ask yourself 'What would be satisfying and appropriate for me?' 'What is it best that I aim for here?' Taking a short time each week and a longer time every month to write out your goals will ensure that you continue to focus on what is important to you.

However well you're doing, there may be days when you feel awful, or when you are faced with sudden changes you weren't bargaining for which totally throw you. You may feel in such a state that the thought of doing anything constructive makes you want to throw the book across the room! This is exactly the time to put your self-esteem information into practice. Remember this upset is an experience you're going through and you will go through it. It is not a permanent condition, although it may feel like that right now.

Even when you've been doing what you can for yourself, when you have felt better and seen improvements, you can suddenly find setbacks or your circumstances will change. Also you are bound to meet and mix with people who may have different agendas to you. This can feel more disappointing initially because you have been doing so well. However, it doesn't mean that things aren't working. Being human you will feel things on an emotional level, whether that is acknowledged or not. Rapid and unexpected changes, particularly if undesired, can throw you, especially where you feel you have no control and your feelings are being disregarded. However, you now know how to help yourself handle any difficult situation. Difficult as it may seem to practise what you have learned at this time, you'll feel more in control and more positive if you apply a sort of first aid for self-esteem!

FIRST AID FOR SELF-ESTEEM

- Take a deep breath and remind yourself that you're safe and well: just tell yourself 'I approve of you, I support you'.

- Let yourself feel what you are feeling, so that your emotions move and change. You can also calm your emotions by doing something physical – going for a walk, doing something in your home or garden. Then, if it's appropriate, just see if you can let go of blaming yourself and the other person or people involved as far as you can.

- What are your most helpful thoughts about yourself and the outcome you want?

- Deliberately describe your situation as just that, not as an emotional upset. Note any practical steps that might help the situation.

- Where you have a person or people that will be supportive, contact them and spend time with them, or you can speak to them on the phone as you need to.

- Excellent as it is to have support from other people, you also need that quiet time to integrate the experience and, even while this is going on, to come back to what is important to you. When you have that feeling of being totally distracted from what is important, focus instead on what will work for you and help you.

- Now really notice what is the kindest thing that you can do for yourself and then do it. It may be to improve your surroundings with flowers, or to take a break for half an hour.

- Remind yourself, *this is an experience you are moving through* and you *can* handle it.

CREATING THE FUTURE YOU WANT

Remember you are at the centre of your life and you have a choice here in what you want to achieve and the kind of person you want to be.

It's important to get to know what you want in your life. You are important, so is your present and your future. Note down your dreams, your daydreams, what appeals to you and what it is you'd love to do. Pay attention to your personal intuition and act on it. It's never too early or too late to create the future you want.

Regardless of the many distractions there are, value and respect yourself enough to focus on what is important to you. Continue to be compassionate to yourself and others. Discovering what is important to you with regard to what you want to do, achieve and be in your life is an ongoing adventure. As you proceed with this you will make the greatest contribution you are capable of. Your life will be satisfying to you and joyful.

Personal Focus

For a Secure and Exciting Future

1 Looking again at your life, what do you most want to achieve for yourself, what sort of person do you want to be? Write this down and include your abilities and good qualities as well as the things you may want – a beautiful home, to travel, a job that makes a contribution. If you want more friends and fun be sure to include that too! Don't concern yourself now about how you will get these, look at the broader picture. Begin making your notes below, continuing in your notebook.

2 Now set goals for achieving your desires, and set these in time frames of, say, two years, two months and two weeks. What are your most important goals? Write these down.

3 What do you need to let go of or change?

4 What thoughts are supportive in your achieving this?

5 Who will support you?

6 Outline the steps you need to take, starting with something you can do in the next day or two.

Keep Your Self-Esteem High

Practise your self-esteem boosters for the next two to three weeks. You might like to set out a programme for yourself, say five to ten minutes daily, at a particular time. Alternate your relaxation time with perhaps looking at new helpful thoughts for yourself, or a session on just letting go of blaming and integrating what you feel. At other times of the day you can simply remember to use any aspect of your self-esteem work when you want to experience the benefits. Draw up your timetable below.

RELAXATION

Moving Forward With Self-Esteeem

Relaxing your body, see and feel yourself secure yet enthusiastic. Feel any worry just dissolving. Notice yourself feeling good, looking good. See your life working for you, notice what you want to achieve and see that happening. Notice what you're doing, who you're with, the kind of surroundings you are in – add plenty of detail. Send out goodwill to smooth your way ahead. Listen to your personal intuition with regard to creating your heart's desire, asking 'What is it important for me to know?' 'What is it important for me to do?' Gently open your eyes. You can note down anything that would be helpful to you.

FINALE

Now that you have worked through this book, you will be able to keep your self-esteem high and give yourself an extra boost when you need it most. Your life can only get better and better. You now know what to do to bring about the changes that are best for you. You can now check on what is appropriate for you by listening to your personal intuition.

It may take some time to get all of the changes you want completed. It takes practice to establish a new way of thinking, feeling and acting. It may also take a while for you to become established in your times of relaxation and self-esteem practice even though you feel the benefits. As you continue with this you will feel balanced and in control however rapid and unexpected the changes in your life.

By listening to your personal intuition, you will know what is best and appropriate for you at any time. You now have the information that will help you and you know how and when to apply it. You can start right away and, as you do, you will feel immediate benefits.

The self-value and self-respect you feel makes it natural for you to respect others and your environment, and take actions that you know are necessary and beneficial.

You will have seen that what is so important in each area of your life is to take into account your specialness, your uniqueness. Your personal intuition is your key to this. What you want is individual to you. You have a special, individual contribution to make. No one else can take your place. Have the courage to move forward with your life. It is by the choices you make, the decisions reached by listening to your personal intuition and the actions you take, that you shape your destiny on a daily basis.

Index

Patricia Cleghorn is Principal of Orchid International, providing Personal Focus programmes for people in business, with one-to-one coaching and group courses.

Our programmes include one that's specially designed for people between the ages of 16–26 called Move Forward With Confidence.

Patricia is Principal of The Self-Esteem Company, providing group seminars as well as one-to-one coaching with specially trained tutors. She is also the author of *30 Minutes ... to Boost Your Self-Esteem*, published by Kogan Page.

Orchid International and The Self-Esteem Company programmes are available throughout Scotland; in London and other areas of the UK; internationally by arrangement.

For information on any of the above programmes, please contact Orchid International/The Self-Esteem Company, PO Box 14749, St Andrews, Scotland KY16 9YT, tel: 44 (0) 1334 470648, email: Orchid2100@aol.com.